Hereward

PETER REX

AMBERLEY

In Memoriam
PETER REX
11 August 1930 – 25 March 2012

This edition first published 2013

Amberley Publishing
The Hill, Stroud
Gloucestershire, GL5 4EP

www.amberleybooks.com

British Library Cataloguing in Publication Data.
A catalogue record for this book is available from the British Library.

ISBN 978 1 4456 0477 0

Typesetting and Origination by Amberley Publishing.
Printed in the UK.

Contents

Foreword

This book, *Hereward: The Last Englishman*, is in some ways a sequel to *The English Resistance: The Underground War against the Normans*. It is presented as a fuller account of the activities and parentage of Hereward, who is presented as '*the last Englishman*', the one who led the last stand against the Conqueror. He represents all those unknown Englishmen who resisted King William and were disinherited, exiled, imprisoned or slain by the Normans.

This book contains an expansion of some material aired in the first book and much new material which, as a result of further research, goes more deeply into the campaign at Ely. It seeks to deal with that contentious issue, the whereabouts of the Conqueror's last and successful assault. It also deals with the claims that the successors to Hereward in some of his lands obtained them by marriage to a succession of heiresses descended from him, showing how improbable and impossible those claims can be said to be. It also attempts to put Hereward more firmly into his Anglo-Danish background.

My grateful thanks go to my wife Christina for her genealogical tables and her ruthless textual criticism; to Dr Janet Fairweather for the use of her translation of the *Liber Eliensis* and to Mike Young for permission

Hereward

to use his excellent maps of the medieval Fens and of Hereward's sojourn in Flanders to illustrate this current edition. I also acknowledge my use of the researches of many scholars, whose works are to be found listed in the Bibliography, and especially the work of Dr Elisabeth van Houts on Hereward in Flanders. These scholars are in no way responsible for the views advanced in this work as a result of their research. Those are entirely my responsibility, as are any errors.

Ely
April 2004
Amended September 2013

Introduction

While it is not possible to produce a full biography of the Lincolnshire thegn called Hereward, the main threads of his career can be recovered, at least in outline. In so doing, the appellation 'Wake' can be disposed of, despite its attachment to his identity by Charles Kingsley, and perhaps his real parentage can be identified.

The more romantic and fantastic elements of the story, largely the invention of twelfth-century storytellers seeking to entertain their audiences, can be eliminated quite simply as matter more suited to the study of literature in the Middle Ages than of history. Only a brief account will therefore be given not only of the twelfth-century inventions but those of later centuries, especially the fourteenth and nineteenth.

The life of Hereward needs to be placed firmly into its eleventh-century context: the Anglo-Danish state that was England in the reign of Edward the Confessor. This entails describing in some detail the extent to which Edwardine England, certainly as far as its governing classes were concerned, was a combination of English and Danish men and influences. This will make it obvious that Hereward, coming, as this account will argue, from a widespread Danish clan, can best be seen as a typical product of the Danish element in the English state. Once the background has been established, evidence can be presented to dispose once and for all of theories about the man based on the suggestion that his father's name was Leofric, and to show that the real clue to his background lies in his relationship to Brand, the last pre-Norman Abbot of Peterborough.

Basing its account on recently published research, and discounting the more fabulous elements in the tales, Hereward's career in exile before the Conquest and during the closing years of King Edward's reign can be told. The argument is that his exploits in Flanders, as described in the *Gesta Herewardi*, are based on real events, and that it was in Flanders that he learned his trade as a soldier, acquiring a sound grounding in the tactics of medieval warfare. From this the pace quickens, as the story is told of his return to England after the Norman Conquest had already taken place, and of his entry onto the stage of history as a leader of a combined Anglo-Danish attack on Peterborough Abbey, an exploit vividly described in the pages of the *Anglo-Saxon Chronicle* and those of the Peterborough Abbey Chronicle of Hugh Candidus.

Events follow thick and fast as Hereward takes refuge on the Isle of Ely, is deserted by his Danish allies and holds out alone until reinforced by the arrival of Earl Morcar of Northumbria and his supporters, and all becoming the focus of William the Conqueror's decision finally to stamp out the last remnants of English resistance. Hereward's career concludes with an attempt to sort out the truth about his final end and the myth of the Wakes is laid to rest.

Some of the traditions about Hereward's exploits after the siege of Ely have quite simply been transferred from their proper place, as part of the account of the attack on Peterborough. These include his conflict with Abbot Turold and possibly his encounters with other opponents such as Ivo Taillebois and William de Warenne. Even the account of a reconciliation with King William may relate to the earlier period, when several leading men submitted to the King; Hereward was simply assumed by later writers to have followed what these others had done.

For his own purposes, Geoffrey Gaimar puts the reconciliation in the context of the war in Maine in which an English contingent certainly took part, and this allows him to present his story of the death of Hereward when set upon by a band of vengeful Normans (as happened to Earl Edwin of Mercia). Was he granting his protagonist a hero's death? The Crowland tradition and the *Gesta Herewardi* contradict Gaimar, and, while also insisting on a reconciliation, Crowland has Hereward retire to his estates which have been restored to him, there to die of old age and be buried. In part this may result from the confusion between Hereward the Lincolnshire Outlaw and another Hereward, who held land in Warwickshire and Worcestershire under the Bishop of Worcester and the Count of Mortain, most of which this man had possessed before 1066 and still held in 1086. The major chronicles simply state that Hereward escaped through the Fens by boat and was never heard of again. Did he, perhaps, simply become one more English exile like so many thousands of others?

The concluding chapters of this book will deal with the question of Hereward's alleged descendants: one set, the Wakes, claim descent in the female line, the other, the Harwards, claim descent in the male line. Neither is convincing. Then the manner in which Hereward has been handled by historians will be considered and, finally, that in which he has been presented by the novelists, starting with Charles Kingsley in 1866. Some account is also given, in an appendix, of what is known about Hereward's companions.

I

The Upper Levels of English Society in the Eleventh Century

In order to understand the kind of man Hereward was, some effort must be made not only to identify his real family background but also to place that background in the context of the English nobility and their role in eleventh-century government. It is a contention of this book that the realm of Edward the Confessor was an Anglo-Danish state in which both men of Anglo-Saxon and of Danish descent regarded themselves as 'English'. That this is so is shown in the pages of the great document usually referred to as the *Anglo-Saxon Chronicle*. The various eleventh/twelfth-century recensions of that work speak of West Saxons and Mercians, of Northumbrians and East Anglians, and Danes, but never a word of 'Anglo-Saxons'. By the eleventh century they were all called 'English folk'. It is further confirmed in the pages of Domesday Book, which speaks of Englishmen and Frenchmen but rarely of Danes, and never of that historical fiction 'Anglo-Saxons'.

Danish Men and Danish Lawgivers

Ever since Alfred's day the numbers of those who could claim Danish blood had been rising. England, like Normandy (the French Danelaw) had a Scandinavian heritage founded on settlement by peoples of Scandinavian origin. Later, men could rightly claim that they came under West Saxon Law or Mercian Law or Dane Law, and a whole area of the country, roughly speaking north and east of Watling Street but excluding north-western Mercia, could be called 'Danelagh'. Indeed, the southern Danelaw was more easily absorbed into England than western Mercia because the Danes had more readily accepted Christianity.

It is there that the Danes had settled intensively, in the land of the Five Boroughs (Derby, Lincoln, Nottingham, Leicester and Stamford), in each of which a Danish army had made its base. As for the area further north, incorporation had been more difficult as kings faced a mixed population of Englishmen, Danes and Irish Norsemen. There they were content to treat the Danes as subjects rather than as conquered people. By the time of Edward the Elder's reign, every shire had its own Ealdorman, though he reduced their numbers to eight south of the Trent, five in the Midlands and East Anglia, and two or three in Wessex, while in the Five Boroughs several men styled themselves 'Eorl' but without official functions. The Ealdormen were leaders of the shire levies in time of war and presided over the shire moots (Stallers acted in this capacity in the eleventh century). Gradually the work of Ealdormen expanded so that they became, in effect, provincial governors ruling a group of shires and so preparing the way for Cnut's creation of the great Earldoms.

In the reign of Aethelraede II Unraede (not 'the Unready' but 'Noble Counsel/Evil Counsel', a pun on his name and meaning 'the Ill-Advised') the Danes had arrived in force and conquered the whole country. This marks the disadvantage of the Anglo-Danish composition of England, in that it made the country attractive to Scandinavian invaders, as did its immense wealth. There was then a short Danish dynasty of three kings, Cnut the Great and his two sons, the half-brothers Harold I Harefoot and Harthacnut, who was rightly said to be only half a Cnut.

Cnut the Great adopted a policy of promoting Danes or men with Danish connections to positions of power and influence. Most of his 'jarls' or earls were in fact Danes, and, of the three great earls who emerged by the end of the reign, Siward of Northumbria was a Dane. Earldoms could be created, enlarged, reduced, or destroyed. The earls remained always the king's military and administrative representatives. They raised the shire levies rather than private armies of retainers, and the courts over which they presided were those of shire and hundred rather than their own private ones. It is a tribute to the strength of this Anglo-Danish monarchy that the two parts of the country, English and Danish, learned to live peacefully together. In eastern England, as Stenton argued, especially in areas of Danish settlement, there developed a new element of freedom in local society which took the form of manors (*mansiones* or *maneria*) consisting of a central estate to which belonged scattered and virtually independent peasants dispersed over a wide area and paying light rents. This explains the frequency with which manors are found to which berewicks and sokes were attached. The essential feature of a manor was the presence of the lord's house, in Old English *heafod botl* or chief dwelling.

It has been suggested that Harthacnut actually prepared the way for Edward the Confessor's succession, making him a sort of joint king and using him as his regent when necessary because he had problems in Denmark and distrusted the earls, but equally it can be argued that he never expected Edward to outlive him. Certainly, the *Anglo-Saxon Chronicle* (the Abingdon Chronicle C, in 1041) says:

And early in the same year came Edward, his brother on his mother's side, from abroad: he was the son of King Aethelraede, and had long been in exile from his country, but nevertheless was sworn in as King: and then he remained in his brother's court as long as he [Harthacnut] lived.

After the death of Harthacnut it would have been possible for any one of the various Danish claimants, Magnus of Norway, Swein Estrithson or Harald Hardrada, to have seized the throne, though it seems none were in the best position to do so. The Anglo-Danish group of earls, led by Earls Godwin and Leofric, saw to it that Edward, recalled to England in the closing months of Harthacnut's reign, was 'received by all folk as king, as was his natural right'. This is usually taken to indicate a desire to return to the Alfredian line of kings, but if so, what made Edward acceptable to the Danes? There is a straightforward answer. Not only was Edward, as son of Aethelraede II, a descendant of the royal house of Cerdic, one of the Woden-born, that is descendants of the God Woden, but also, through his mother, Emma, daughter of Richard I, Duke of Normandy, descended from that Rollo or Rolf, the Viking, who had founded Normandy (the Frankish Danelaw). So Edward was also of Scandinavian descent. Only three generations separate the two; Edward was Rolf's great-great-grandson. This cannot have gone unnoticed or uncommented upon during his sojourn in Normandy.

A further indication of the Anglo-Danish nature of the English state is that Earl Godwin of Wessex had married into the Danish Royal Family. His wife Gytha was sister to Ulf of Denmark, brother-in-law of Cnut. Of the other earls, only Leofric, Earl of Mercia, was English, son of Ealdorman Leofwine. Intermarriage was common, and among the upper classes, important. Some prominent examples make the point. Edmund had married a Danish widow, which helped him to recover the loyalty of the Five Boroughs; Cnut the Great himself married, albeit according to the Danish custom, 'more Danico', that is without Christian marriage, Aelfgyfu 'of Northampton', daughter of Ealdorman Aelfhelm; and the House of Bamburgh (the descendants of the previous rulers of Northumbria) was of mixed Danish and English blood. Leofwine, Ealdorman of Mercia and father of Earl Leofric, named his elder son Northman, perhaps because his wife was a Danish woman. Thorkell the Tall's wife was named Edith: perhaps she was Aethelraede's daughter?

King's Thegns

There were Danes, too, among the ranks of the king's thegns: those who held 'seat and special duty' in the King's Hall, and served as his eyes and ears in the shires. There were two ranks of such king's thegns, those of ordinary rank (the Median Thegns) and those 'who stand nearest to him'. In general, when royal writs are addressed to the bishop and sheriff (shire-reeve) and 'to all my thegns in Norfolk' (for example), the word 'King's' (cynges) is to be understood before the word 'thegns'. The Latin equivalents were 'minister' and even 'miles'. They were the king's personal 'men' from whom he might select his earls. They attended Witenagemots (meetings of the king's council) but otherwise did not necessarily hold a specific office. Wulfric Spot, for example, owner of over seventy villages and founder of Burton Abbey, had inherited most of his land. He had no definite duties but always felt free to speak his mind.

Thus king's thegns were a numerous class, and some of these thegns were wealthy men, well equipped for war. Indeed, by the eleventh century, the word 'thegn' itself could imply nobility, as in the *Document Dunsaete* cap. 5, which states that the law applies to men 'whether thegn-born or ceorl-born' and the distinction is borne out by the difference in wergild. A thegn of ordinary rank had a wergild of 1,200 shillings (a twelfth-hyndman) and a ceorl (or peasant) had one of only 200 shillings. In the North wergilds were expressed in 'thrymsas' (worth 3 Mercian pennies) so that a hold (a title derived from that of army leaders ranking immediately below the jarl) or a king's high reeve was valued at 4,000, a thegn at 2,000 and a ceorl at 266 (=200 shillings). Wergild was the amount due to be paid for slaying a man. By the 1060s charters were using 'princeps' for these major thegns, those with higher status, which again suggested nobility.

The rank of thegn became hereditary, but a man might thrive and better himself until he held 'fully five hides of his own land, church and kitchen, bell house and burh gate, seat and special duty in the king's hall, then he was thenceforth thegnright worthy'. He might prosper even more and come to serve the king at his summons and among his household, a plain definition of a king's thegn who might even become an earl. The references in Domesday Book to 'huscarls', the Danish fully trained household troops, should not be overlooked either, though such a man corresponded closely to the Old English rank of thegn. The main difference was that some huscarls formed a highly organised guild of specialised fighting men.

All these men were expected to be well equipped for war, as documents listing their 'heriot' show. A man's heriot was his military equipment, which reverted to his lord at his death. A law of Cnut laid down that an earl's heriot was eight horses (four saddled and four unsaddled), four helmets, four coats of mail, eight spears and eight shields, four swords and two hundred mancuses of gold. A king's thegn nearest to the king surrendered four horses (two saddled and two unsaddled), four spears, four shields, two swords, one helmet and one coat of mail and fifty mancuses of gold. The middling thegn gave up a horse and its trappings and his arms (that is, one of everything). Furthermore, among the Danes, a king's thegn who 'had his soke' (sundry rights of legal jurisdiction) had a heriot of four pounds, but if closer to the king, two horses (one saddled and one not), a sword, two spears, two shields and fifty mancuses of gold (=1,500 silver pennies).

These king's thegns were men with estates in several shires, equivalent in size and value to a Norman barony. For instance, Aelfstan of Boscombe in Wiltshire had lands in eight shires, forfeited after the Conquest and forming the major part of the barony of William, Count of Eu. Such were the men who served the king, and he regarded it as necessary to maintain their dignity in order to safeguard the honour of the Crown. By the reign of King Edward many of these royal servants were known by the Scandinavian title of staller or place-holder (another indication that the English state had become Anglo-Danish), implying that he was a permanent member of the royal entourage.

In the Danelaw before the Conquest, and particularly in Lincolnshire, society possessed a high degree of freedom. Land was held by thegns and sokemen with free disposal of their estates (that is, they could be held, as Domesday Book said of Asketil, brother of Abbot Brand, '*in propria libertate*'). They performed service in the Wapentake, in person. *Sake* and *soke* implied a whole range of judicial dues, food rents, labour services, all reserved for the holder of the soke, the overlord, who was answerable directly to the king. Sake and soke were held together with *toll* and *team* (the right to receive payment from the sale of goods within an estate and to hold a court to settle disputes over cattle or goods) and often *infangenetheof* (the right to hang a thief caught red-handed with stolen goods). The possession of sake and soke was indicative also of the ownership of Bookland, held by the possession of a landbook or charter.

Such king's thegns, because they were seen as overlords of lesser men, were to be considered by the makers of Domesday Book to be the designated predecessors of the new Norman owners, and several are listed as conferring title on their successors. King's thegns holding groups of dependent manors were seen by the Normans to resemble lords holding by barony; they could be personally summoned to the *fyrd* and be held responsible for seeing that their 'men' performed military service just like a baron being summoned to the host and being held responsible for the performance of military service by his knights. Indeed, it could be said that a *fief* had many of the characteristics of Bookland and that an honorial baron was a king's thegn in all but name.

Whether such overlordship was common is still a matter of debate. Some argue that there were many more than are named in Domesday but that they must have existed, as it was from such men that the Norman successors derived their title to land. Others deny this, maintaining that the absence of such named overlords shows that such overlordship was not prevalent. But there is evidence that some Norman 'honours' did in fact derive from the lands of a single English overlord. This does not eliminate the idea that elsewhere estates belonging to several different individuals were put together to form a holding for a particular Norman. Generally speaking, the nebulous bonds of commendation and soke were replaced by the Norman concept of enfeoffment with land in return for military service. In practice the lands of king's thegns were forfeited to King William because they had fought against him or rebelled and he made use of the English rule that the lands of king's thegns could only be forfeited to the king. Another indication of overlordship was the existence of multiple manors formed of groups of estates under one lord. That the overlord was not always named is explained because the holders of sake and soke were not always named if the land was held by tenants under them.

The exact proportions of men of English or Danish origin cannot be known and certainly there was much intermarriage, so that a man with an English or Danish personal name might not be wholly of one race. By 1066 there were landowners in every part of England with Scandinavian names, many of whom had inherited their land from men who had served Cnut. Ansgar the Staller, for example, was grandson of Cnut's man Tovi the Proud. Other men richly endowed with wide lands and bearing Danish names include Colegrim, Haelfdan Topeson, his brother Ulf Topeson and Toki of Lincoln, whose Norman successor in almost all his lands was the baron Geoffrey Alselin. Some indication of proportions can be gained from lists of personal names used in those areas for which lists exist; these are Northamptonshire, where one third are Danish, North Cambridgeshire, with fifty per cent, and South Yorkshire, about two thirds. Scandinavian name forms were still in use in Henry II's time, with hundreds in Yorkshire and Lincolnshire, scores in Nottinghamshire, Derbyshire and Norfolk, and more in Leicestershire, Northamptonshire and Suffolk. Elsewhere they are rarer.

Royal Power

Such were the kind of ruling classes with which Edward the Confessor had to contend as king. Always he had to deal with men representing the traditions of Cnut's Anglo-Danish monarchy and yet he was accepted as king by this formidable group of Anglo-Danish warriors and statesmen. Surrounded as he was by such 'servants', it is no wonder that he sought solace in the companionship of men with whom he had been acquainted in Normandy and among whom he had grown up. This alone, rather than any deep laid plot to 'Normanise' England or prepare the way for the accession of William the Bastard, explains his desire to have the company of 'Frenchmen'.

The Anglo-Danish state was the work of Cnut the Great and it was merely the Old English state under new direction. Huscarls linked localities to the Danish king just as the English king's thegns had done. Many of the older aristocracy had been destroyed in the battles, to be replaced by English and Danish parvenus. During his reign, Cnut remained, like William I after him, a conqueror. His authority rested on military force not blood-right, again like William, and Danish blood-right did not succeed in establishing itself because Cnut's sons lacked his abilities. So the Old English dynasty was restored for a time, leaving open the question whether the Old English state had also been restored. This book argues that the state ruled by Edward was still the Anglo-Danish creation of Cnut the Great, doomed to be destroyed by the Normans.

Cnut took steps to ensure good government – lacking in Aethelraede's reign – accepting baptism and the unction of a Christian king to ensure the support of the Church, and promoting pro-Danish English earls (though in the less important parts of his realm, at least at first, until they had proved themselves to his satisfaction). There was no systematic forfeiture of lands or offices, though an abundant sprinkling of Scandinavians and their followers was endowed in southern England, in effect forming a garrison. At the Great Moot at Oxford in 1019 he declared that he would rule by the law of Edgar, and thereafter continued and fostered English traditions.

So effective were his policies that he was able to leave the country for many months during the first three years of his reign and it never became necessary to use the force he possessed to hold down the country, unlike the Conqueror. This institution of monarchy continued to receive the respect which was its due, and this ultimate respect for it prevented the outbreak of actual civil war during Edward's reign. Cnut had achieved this by refraining from antagonising the English, accepting and maintaining the existing historical boundaries and the traditions of local autonomy as the basis of his government. The trend towards governing groups of shires through ealdormen continued, even though the title changed to that of earl, and in the early part of the reign up to a dozen earls are to be found in office.

A small Scandinavian aristocracy formed around the King, mainly related to Cnut himself by kinship or marriage. (Bernicia was restricted to the area between Tees and Tweed, under the High Reeves of Bamburgh and supervised by the Danish Earl Siward. East Anglia, Hereford, Worcestershire and Yorkshire went to the care of Scandinavians.) So effective was the system created by Cnut, a combination of the existing Old English administration under ealdormen, sheriffs and king's thegns and reeves with Cnut's own contribution, the provincial earldoms, that under Edward the existence of the several earldoms proved no threat to the kingdom's political unity and there was never any hint that Edward might be removed.

Edward did indeed force the Godwinsons to flee the country, but he was unable to keep them out where a more forceful ruler might have done so. Cnut had no such problems and never allowed his earls to become the equivalent of dukes or counts as on the continent. They kept the names of the old tribal areas – Wessex, Mercia, Northumbria – but not their boundaries. Wessex was confined south of the Thames, Mercia no longer ran from the Welsh border to the North Sea nor Northumbria to the Firth of Forth. Nor was the title of earl so nearly, but not quite, hereditary as to allow the consolidation of lands with their own officials and administration such as occurred in Western Europe.

It was this Danish state and background into which, probably some time after 1045, Hereward was born. His name is Danish. It is the contention of this work that he was born into a well-to-do Danish family and that his father was a king's thegn. It is this Danish background which accounts for his alliance with the Danes in 1070 and which undermines Douglas Jerrold's accusation (*An Introduction to the History of England*, 1949) that he was a 'quisling'. Jerrold defines a quisling as 'a political anti-nationalist' who sees 'the best future for his country lies in ceasing to be an independent nation state'. This is a poor definition, and meaningless for the eleventh century, when there were no 'independent nation states' in the modern sense. In any case, Vidkun Quisling of Norway was a collaborator who accepted the position of head of government in German-occupied Norway, a traitor by anyone's standard. His equivalent in Norman England must be sought in the ranks of those who accepted the Conqueror as king and aided him in governing the country, men like Archbishop Ealdred of York, Bishop Wulfstan of Worcester or Abbot Aethelwig of Evesham.

That he might have preferred a Dane to a Norman as king, as would thousands of others both English and Danish, does not make Hereward a traitor. Even in eleventh-century terms, Hereward had not accepted William as his lord and king and was quite free to fight against him. Hereward and those like him who fought the Normans did not see themselves as desiring the return of 'alien', that is 'foreign', rule, because to them it was William and his 'Frenchmen' who were the foreigners.

2

Hereward:
The Myths about his Parentage

The Problem of Hereward's Ancestry

All the sources agree that Hereward was (a) Lord of Bourne and (b) son of a man called Leofric of Bourne and his wife Aediva. The problem is twofold. As Domesday Book testifies, the pre-Conquest Lord of Bourne was Morcar, Earl of Northumbria:

> The men of Aveland Wapentake bear witness that in King Edward's Time the Manor of Bourne belonged to Earl Morcar.

This is quite unequivocal and disposes of any suggestion that Morcar only held the manor because Hereward had forfeited it. It is almost as though the men testifying at the Wapentake (the local court) are determined to reject claims that anyone else held Bourne (in Lincolnshire) before the Conquest. Domesday Book twice refers to Hereward's flight (into exile) when stating that certain lands did not belong to him before 1066. In neither case does it specifically say that the lands were forfeit as part of the punishment of outlawry, though this is probably the case. Nor does the Wapentake, as one might expect, include Bourne as part of Hereward's land or say that he had forfeited it before fleeing. Some historians do try to argue that Morcar might have been holding Bourne because it had been forfeited by Hereward, though it is admitted that Domesday Book does not show that Hereward held Bourne. The attribution of Bourne to Hereward probably derives from the fact that his successor, in lands at Rippingale, Ringstone, Laughton, Aslackby and Avethorpe, all near Bourne, was Ogier the Breton, who also acquired the lordship of Bourne. Morcar's land holdings in Lincolnshire were somewhat questionable and he did not always have full rights over lands attributed to him, notably Castle Bytham, which the will of Ulf Topeson shows belonged to Ulf.

Bourne might have been attributed to Morcar because it was part of his Earldom. Certainly Drogo de la Bevrière claimed Bourne because he held Castle Bytham, though the Wapentake denied his claim. All claims to Morcar's lands were left for the king to settle. A more logical and simple explanation would be to say firstly that Bourne was the chief seat (Caput) of the Bourne fief of Ogier the Breton, son of Ungomar. It included the soke of Bourne and other sokelands in Rippingale, Laughton, Kilsby and Thrapstone. Then, secondly, Ogier was Hereward's successor in estates around Bourne, and therefore the twelfth-century writers jumped to the conclusion that Bourne had also belonged to Ogier's 'antecessor', Hereward.

Why Leofric?

The second problem is that no one called 'Leofric of Bourne' can be identified. Such a mode of identification is commonly used in Domesday to identify king's thegns, men such as Edric 'of Laxfield', Aethelwig 'of Thetford' or Asketil 'of Ware'. There is no Leofric 'of Bourne' nor any other king's thegn so named, though a middle-ranking man of that name does hold a few parcels of land in Lincolnshire and elsewhere. *A fortiori*, Hereward was not, as Charles Kingsley and others have made him, son of Earl Leofric of Mercia. The earl's son, and grandsons, are well enough known: Aelfgar, Earl of East Anglia, who succeeded his father as Earl of Mercia in 1057 and died in 1062 or 1063, and his sons; Burgheard, who died in 1061 at Rheims, and the Earls Edwin and Morcar.

Aelfgar, the only and real son of Earl Leofric, who had no brother, was twice exiled by King Edward and accused of treason, and that might explain the notion that Hereward, who was also exiled, because he 'stirred up sedition among the people' (*Gesta Herewardi*), was Leofric's son. Aelfgar's death is not actually recorded – he simply disappears from sources in 1062 after the death of his son Burgheard. Some have suggested his involvement in more disturbances and that his death might explain the silence of the chronicles. But there are gaps in the chronicles during this period. However, such troubles might suggest a context for Hereward's outlawry.

The two sources which insist that Hereward's father was Leofric of Bourne are the *Gesta Herewardi*, from the twelfth century but extant in a thirteenth-century manuscript and the *History of Crowland Abbey*, from the fourteenth. They are really, for much of their material, only one source, as the second is dependent upon a source very similar to the *Gesta*. A comparison of the two accounts in table form shows the relationship and exposes the errors in both.

Gesta Version	**Crowland Version**
Father: Leofric of Bourne	*Leofric, Lord of Bourne*
Leofric is son of Earl Ralf,	*nepos of Radin, Earl of*
Surnamed Scabre or Scalre	*Hertford whose wife is*
	Goda, sister of King
	Edward

| Mother: Aedina who is great-great-granddaughter of Duke Oslac | Aediva who is niece of Duke Oslac |

The two accounts contradict each other and are riddled with errors.

In the *Gesta* version Ralf Scabre is meant to be Ralph the Staller (Scalre in Rolls series edition), the half-Breton minister of King Edward, and Earl of East Anglia after the Conquest. Certainly no son of his was called Leofric.

Duke Oslac of Northumbria was prominent in King Edgar's reign, flourishing in 966, and his relationship to 'Aediva' is not impossible. There is no way otherwise of identifying her. The Rolls series edition of the text gives her name as Aedina '*trinepta Oslaci ducis*'. In the Crowland account she is impossibly stated to be Oslac's niece.

In this account Leofric is now a '*nepos*' of Earl Radin or (as some texts of the manuscript state) Ralph 'of Hertford', which is a mistake of misreading for 'Hereford', but Ralph of Hereford was Edward's nephew Ralph of Mantes, and Goda (or Gytha) was his mother not his wife. He married a namesake of his mother called 'Gethe' or Countess Gueth (which looks Welsh). 'Earl Ralph' (whether of East Anglia or of Hereford) certainly did not have a son or other relation called Leofric, which is, in any case, an English name, not one of Danish origin.

Such errors destroy the credibility of the Crowland account as an independent source and weaken the authority of the *Gesta* on such a crucial matter. As has been well said, 'heroes need illustrious ancestors', and these writers do their best to supply them. The reference to Ralph the Staller may reflect the Ely tradition that Hereward was involved in the rebellion of the earls (Ralph Guader, Earl of East Anglia in succession to his father, and Roger, Earl of Hereford) in 1075.

Although there is a man called Leofric who held land in Lincolnshire and elsewhere in 1066, he cannot be shown to have any connection, familial or territorial, with Hereward. A search for Hereward's parentage must look elsewhere.

Hereward's Lands and Status

Whoever his father was, Hereward was certainly a man of some means before his exile. David Roffe, in his essay on the Bourne barony, has argued persuasively for Hereward's high social standing, which has been denied by some historians, notably Round, Freeman and Hart, and accepted uncritically by others, such as Kingsley and Bevis. Gaimar claims nobility for him and later sources eventually make him an earl's son. The *Peterborough Chronicle* introduces him as participant in a story so well known as to require no further explanation of who he was. Domesday Book has much to say about him and it is worth reviewing the estates attributed to him to provide a clue about his social status. His lands lie north, west and south-west of, but not in, Bourne. Several estates are listed under the holding of Peterborough Abbey, which held some before and several after 1066. Lands in Domesday Book are given a valuation for tax purposes. Such values are usually given either in 'hides' of 120 acres in southern England, or in 'carucates' containing eight 'bovates'. These are not, by the eleventh century, actual measures of area but more like rateable values; each estate was rated at so many hides or carucates and the king's tax, the geld, was levied on it at so many shillings to the hide or carucate. The productivity of an estate is better estimated from the values in pounds and shillings found at the end of entries.

Hereward's property was in Witham-on-the-Hill and Manthorpe along with Toft and Lound. There he held

twelve bovates of land to the geld and there were one-and-
a-half ploughs. Its 1086 population was twelve men, and
Abbot Turold of Peterborough's man Ansfrid was the new
holder. Ansfrid also held a berewick (or outlying portion)
of this estate at Barholme and Stowe. This was rated at
one carucate (=eight bovates) and four men farmed it.
Sokeland of the Abbey at Stowe in Barholme was rated at
four-and-a-half bovates and farmed by three men. There
were also some sokelands belonging to the abbey, and
held by Ansfrid, rated at one carucate and held by two
of Turold's men, Geoffrey and Robert. There were three
peasants and nine sokemen farming this estate. Ansfrid
also held another berewick in Witham itself, rated at half
a carucate (=four bovates) farmed by fourteen men, and
a soke in Stowe rated at two bovates. It looks as though
Ansfrid, identified elsewhere as a 'man' of the Norman
Abbot Turold, was Hereward's successor as tenant of the
abbey. Hugh Candidus and several Peterborough surveys
call this man Asfort (Old Norse *Asfrothr*).

If Hereward held the whole lot, including berewicks
and sokelands, he had four carucates and six-and-a-half
bovates in the Witham area. These lands were valued
at £3 8s 4d. The next significant entry is at Laughton.
There Hereward held an estate jointly with a man called
Toli (who also held one carucate in Billingham). It was
not unusual for brothers to hold land in this way and
although it is neither impossible nor open to proof,
this Toli (which is also a Danish name) could be the
brother whom the *Gesta* account alleges was killed by
the Normans, but equally could have been a partner
with, or a tenant holding land from, Hereward. The land
at Laughton was rated at four bovates, farmed by four
men, and worth 40s. Another six bovates in Aslackby
and Avethorpe were a berewick of Laughton farmed
by two men. These lands were later held by Ogier the
Breton who is usually reckoned as Hereward's 'Norman'

successor. It may also be the case that another carucate
of land in Laughton held by Ogier is also part of the
original holding, which would total two carucates and
two bovates there.

Other lands are then attributed to Ogier which,
according to the 'Clamores' or complaints section at the
end of the Lincolnshire entries, were also associated with
Hereward. Firstly, in Ringstone and Rippingale, Ogier held
one carucate, with another carucate in Ringstone itself.
Then in Rippingale there were three carucates set aside by
'St Guthlac', that is Crowland Abbey, for the sustenance
of the monks, and this was now held by Ogier. Part of
the land was farmed by three sokemen who owed suit
of court to the abbey. In 1066 it had been valued at 40s.
It was Ogier who now also held Bourne, Earl Morcar's
manor, rated at two-and-a-half carucates and worth
£5. This manor had a berewick in Dyke rated at seven
bovates. In total Hereward appears to have held just over
twelve carucates. There is very little known about Ogier,
but the available details are that he witnesses a charter of
Count Alan for Swavesey in around 1086 as *Oger filius
Vngemar*, and is the father of Ralph and Conan. He was
succeeded by Ralph well before 1130.

Ogier appears to have held some seven carucates which
had once belonged, some only briefly, to Hereward. If
other estates held by Ogier are added, then Hereward
held some twelve carucates, the equivalent, according to
F. M. Stenton, of two six-carucate units, each furnishing
sustenance for one fully armed man, the Danelaw
equivalent of the five hide units (a thegn's holding) found
in some of the shires of southern England. Stenton pointed
to Barholme and Stowe which, with its dependent estates,
all belonging to Peterborough, amounted to a vill of six
carucates. If Hereward held a total of twelve carucates,
then he too had two six-carucate units, each providing
one armed man for the fyrd.

Reference to the Clamores provides two allusions to Hereward's flight from the country in the context of lands held by him before the Conquest. Several writers have preferred to take all the references to his flight as applying to the period after the fall of Ely, but the texts in the Clamores do not seem to support this. Having asserted that the Wapentake of Aveland bears witness that Bourne belonged to Earl Morcar T.R.E. (that is, 'in King Edward's Time') the account moves to consider various disputes concerning the holdings of Ogier the Breton. Here it sets out the situation regarding the three carucates in Rippingale set aside for the monks' sustenance as follows:

> The Wapentake of Aveland say that St. Guthlac's land, which Ogier holds in Rippingale, was the monks' demesne farm, and that Abbot Ulfcytel granted it to 'Hereweard' at farm, as might be agreed between them each year; but the abbot took possession of it again before Hereweard fled the country, because he had not kept to the agreement.

This cannot refer to 1071 after the fall of Ely as Hereward by then was already an outlaw and in no position to make tenancy agreements with anybody. It surely better fits the time when Ulfcytel became abbot in his own right, after the end of Abbot Leofric of Peterborough's superintendence of Crowland and several other monasteries granted to him by King Edward, that is 1062. Ulfcytel in some sources is said to have been made abbot in 1051, but that may have been as a kind of deputy to Leofric of Peterborough. As will be seen, 1062 fits very nicely into an account of Hereward's pre-Conquest activities.

The last reference is a brief note by the Ness Wapentake that:

Hereweard did not have Asfort's land in Barholme
Hundred on the day on which he fled.

As before, Hereward the hunted outlaw, a refugee on
the Isle of Ely, would not have been thought of as a
landowner back in Lincolnshire. The land in question
would appear to be the carucate of land in Barholme
and Stowe forming a berewick of Hereward's estate at
Witham-on-the-Hill etc. which had been granted to Abbot
Turold's man Ansfrid or Asfrith (he is also called Asfort
in other documents and his estates confirm his identity;
his actual name was probably Asfrothr) who had also
been granted Hereward's lands at Witham-on-the-Hill.
Are these possibly the four-and-a-half bovates at Stowe
which were also granted to this man? Other references to
Barholme and Stowe do not mention the Abbot's man.

A further point can be made about Hereward's
Rippingale agreement. It fits the pattern of a thegn of
sufficient rank to be thought suitable to become the
Advocate or Protector of a monastery. If, as Hugh
Candidus of Peterborough insists, Hereward was 'a man
of the monks', holding land as a tenant of Peterborough
Abbey, Ulfcytel might well have thought it wise to try
to make him a 'man' of Crowland also. David Roffe
argues rather that Hereward was more likely to have
been a king's thegn (or as this work will argue, the son
of a very prominent and powerful king's thegn) because
of the terms on which he, briefly, held Rippingale. He
was to hold it at an annual rental by agreement with the
abbot rather than in the manner in which lesser, median,
thegns were granted land by religious houses. Such men
regularly received grants but on heavy terms requiring
annual services and fulfilment of the three public burdens
of military ('fyrd') service, and work on the fortresses
('burhs') and bridges. Monasteries needed the protection
of powerful local thegns against encroachments by

local families. Perhaps Crowland felt the need for a local patron and turned to Hereward because of his connection, through Abbot Brand, with Peterborough. He might have held his estates from Peterborough also as 'advocate' or protector, which would explain the way in which he justified the sacking of Peterborough, 'out of fealty to the Church'. Such a role would have needed the support of a powerful kindred, which is just what Hereward apparently had, until his behaviour finally exhausted his father's patience.

Hereward became troublesome to the authorities (perhaps his treatment of Ulfcytel was part of the pattern of youthful wildness implied by the *Gesta*) and 'at the request of his father' he was exiled by King Edward 'for stirring up sedition among the populace and tumult among the common people' as the *Gesta* says. The sources are silent as to the circumstances.

So far it has been established that Hereward was a Lincolnshire thegn, potentially a prosperous landowner. He held some of his land as the tenant of Peterborough Abbey and his holdings are listed either as belonging to the abbey or given by Abbot Turold to his 'man' Asfort, or granted by the king to Ogier the Breton in 1086. Hereward's status was close to that of a king's thegn since, had he not been exiled, he would surely have succeeded to the status of his father along with his estates. If, as is suggested here, his father was a king's thegn, this would account for his relationship to Ogier, as his designated predecessor. Ogier held Laughton and its soke. Laughton was a multiple manor and of such holdings Domesday frequently records the name of the overlord, in this case, Hereward. In addition, he had been the holder, at least for a time, of Ogier's other estate of Rippingale. Ogier's title to Rippingale derived from Hereward despite the abbey's claim that Hereward had forfeited it before the Conquest. Hereward is not listed among those in Lincolnshire possessing sake and soke, but, as will be argued below, his father was. If Hereward had not possessed sufficient status to be regarded as an overlord, then Ogier as tenant-in-chief would not have had a presumptive right to the manor beyond merely appropriating it.

The terms of Hereward's tenancy at Rippingale were honourable, much lighter than those considered binding on a median thegn, and this gives credence to the idea that Hereward, albeit briefly, had been the advocate or protector of Crowland.

The Man Himself

Some may wonder what sort of a man Hereward was, beyond what is said of his fighting abilities and his quality as a leader of men. No portrait exists, but the *Gesta Herewardi* offers a short description:

> Short, stoutly made, agile, with long golden hair, an oval face, with eyes light in colour and not matched.

In other words, a fairly typical English warrior of the eleventh century. His dress and appearance, when not equipped for war, would have been that attributed to the English by William of Malmesbury: a short garment reaching mid-knee, his beard shaven (but possibly the face moustachioed), arms laden with gold bracelets and skin punctured with designs (tattoos). Among his other, non-military, talents was the ability to sing and play the harp 'after the manner of the Girvii', that is the tribe called the Gyrwe living on the western edge of the Fens and from whom the Fenlanders were descended. The two divisions of this tribe were each assigned possession of 600 hides in a document of the tenth century called the Tribal Hidage, reflecting the existence of provinces or regions in England in earlier centuries.

Nothing is known of Hereward's actual birth or early youth, though tradition reckoned him to have been eighteen years of age when he fled. If that was 1063 then he would have been born in around 1045. It can be assumed that he grew up on his father's estates and lived the typical life of the time. He would surely, in addition to his learning the harp, have engaged in the hunting pursuits of the time, hawking and boar hunting, and in due course, as a thegn's son, would have been trained in the arts of fighting with javelin, axe and sword. He would seem to have been a fine horseman, as his later career demonstrates. As a youth living on the margin of the Fens he was also acquainted with the skills required to move among the Fens by water and probably went hunting for game, especially waterfowl.

As a 'man' of Peterborough, Hereward was probably again more than a mere tenant among others, especially in view of his relationship to Abbot Brand. His status enabled Hugh Candidus to justify his attack on the abbey. He is seen as entitled to act as he did, '*pro fidelitate ecclesie*', out of fealty to the church. This amounted to more than mere commendation, and bound a man more closely to his lord while recognising his status as a free man. In return the faithful man (termed 'thegn' in England rather than the continental term 'vassal') received a benefice, usually land. In return the man gives aid to his lord and is expected to defend him. (Hereward later would not have regarded Turold as a legitimate successor to Abbot Brand, seeing him as a usurper.)

He appears in the surviving accounts of his activities as a real person, not some kind of idealised or sanitised hero. He is ruthless in war, though he has learnt some of the chivalrous customs prevalent in Flanders. Thus, he is credited with releasing defeated opponents who present no threat and even with accepting ransom. But he would readily use fire. In Scaldemariland he was ready to burn the ambassadors sent by the people there to negotiate a settlement and did in fact burn the wagons and baggage train of the enemy.

When his own men expressed doubts about the wisdom of continuing the struggle at Ely he is said to have lost his temper:

> At this Hereward rose up, and confronting them head-on, fell upon them; some he struck down, others he despatched to death in the water, and that day, he thus rescued his men from fear.

Into the mouth of the knight Deda, the author of the *Liber Eliensis* puts the following testimony to him:

> Their leader is Hereward, a man in the prime of life and one who has in all respects been most energetic in warfare ever since his youth; among free men he is by no means of low rank where nobility or riches are concerned.

And he adds that:

> It is at the hands of these men (Hereward and those with him) that all the king's men and liegemen who have engaged in sword fights with them have perished; and they are continuing ceaselessly to perpetrate slaughter and pillage all around the kingdom.

Deda concludes that the king must either defeat them or

> admit them to your love as people in harmony with your sovereignty.

Elsewhere Hereward is described as '*strenuis*' or as a '*vir strenuissimus*', a vigorous or most strenuous man, that is full of knightly vigour, the '*miles in armis strenuis*' or fully trained knight. Yet to many of the monastic writers, especially those whose monasteries had suffered at his hands, he is nothing but a thief. The portrait is certainly 'warts and all'.

Fire raising was certainly one of his most characteristic methods of warfare. He used fire against the enemy in Scaldemariland, and later fired three vills near Witham-on-the-Hill as a signal to summon his men to action. Fire was his means of entry in the attack at Peterborough via the Bolhithe Gate. He set fire to Burwell and, most formidably, set ablaze the Fen and burnt King William's siege towers. Before reluctantly quitting Ely, he was only with difficulty persuaded not to set light to the town and the monastery, so that they should not fall intact into William's hands. His men left at Stuntney to cover the retreat were also told to use fire.

3

His Real Family Background

That Peterborough held on to several estates linked to Hereward demonstrates the truth of the assertion that he was 'a man of the monks'. There is no connection with any 'Manor of Bourne', nor was his father called Leofric of Bourne, let alone was he Earl of Mercia. To find his parentage it is necessary to look elsewhere, and fortunately there are several much-overlooked clues.

According to two, admittedly very late, sources, Hereward was the nephew of Abbot Brand, but the truth of that claim is perhaps supported by the fact that lands belonging to Hereward were among those preserved for the abbey by that abbot when he managed to persuade King William to confirm the abbey's ownership of the lands of his relatives and kinsmen (Writ No. 8 in the *Regesta Anglo-Normannorum*). If being Brand's nephew is true then, logically, Hereward's father must be a brother of the abbot. Several well-founded sources provide not one but four brothers; Asketil, Siric, Siworth and Godric. All but the last have Danish names.

Those historians who mention the relationship of Hereward and Brand do not dispute it. It is not the sort of detail a medieval writer would invent, particularly if seeking to establish that Hereward had noble parents. Both sources which give this information just throw it in. The first test comes from the *History of Crowland Abbey*, which is usually referred to as the work of Ingulf. The text purports to have been written by Abbot Ingulf, who succeeded Ulfcytel after his deposition and held the abbacy at the end of the eleventh century. For many years after the *History* was discovered it was believed to be what it claimed to be but modern scholars, citing the many errors and chronological inconsistencies, as well as the author's propensity for garbling his sources (his Latin was poor and his Old English worse), have redated it to around 1350 by an unknown monk of Crowland who preferred to hide his ignorance behind the name of a famous predecessor. New Testament scholars would call the work pseudepigraphical, written under a predecessor's name to borrow his authority for what the real author had to say.

There has been some reassessment of the text in recent years and it is no longer dismissed as complete fabrication. Indeed, some of its sources can themselves be identified. One of those sources was a document close to, if not quite identical with, Robert of Swaffham's text of the *Gesta Herewardi*. But the *Gesta* does not say that Brand was Hereward's uncle, whereas 'Ingulf' incongruously does, not once but twice. He first gives the erroneous family background for Hereward, discussed earlier, and then describes how, on his return from exile, he asked his uncle Abbot Brand to make him a knight. A little later on he records Brand's death and again calls him 'the uncle of Hereward'. The question then arises: how could Brand, a Dane, be the paternal uncle (*patruus*) of a man alleged to be son of an English thegn? Leofric of Bourne was not Hereward's father, but Brand certainly could be his uncle.

In claiming that Abbot Brand was Hereward's uncle, Ingulf might have been reporting an item of local tradition. Most of the rest of the text is derived from the *Gesta*.

He says that the 'earls', now at Ely, summoned Hereward to their aid but his account of what happened there is totally confused. Like the *Liber Eliensis*, Ingulf mixes up the resistance at Ely with the revolt of the earls in 1075, telescoping the two into one. He also calls Hereward himself an earl, which may be the origin of the idea that his alleged father, Leofric, was the Earl of Mercia.

The second reference is found in the *Chronicle of the Abbot John* (of Peterborough), perhaps more accurately known as *Annales Burgo-Spaldenses*, the only copy of which was published by Joseph Sparke in 1723. The entries relevant to Hereward can be found as footnotes in W. T. Mellows' edition of the *Chronicle of Hugh Candidus*. They take the form of annals, that is references to notable events intended to mark particular years as an aide-memoire. The relevant entry, which is also the earliest reference to Hereward as 'le Wake', runs as follows:

> There died Brand, Abbot of Peterborough, paternal uncle (patruus) of the said Hereward le Wake, to whom by the King's choice there succeeded Turold.

The use of '*patruus*' is very important. In Latin an uncle is either paternal, on the father's side, or maternal (*matruus*) on the mother's side. If Brand is his paternal uncle then it is among Brand's brothers that Hereward's father is to be found. It is significant that the entry is telling us something about Brand and not directly about Hereward; he is that Brand who was Hereward's uncle and was succeeded by Turold. The date of death and the name of his successor are both accurate, as are most other references to Hereward and Turold (or, if erroneous, so was the source of the annal). There is no reason to suppose that the writer, or his source, thought the reference to Hereward was anything but fact also. There is some confirmation of these conjectures in the fact that those lands associated with Hereward which did not fall into the hands of Ogier, that is those he held as a man of the Peterborough monks, were among those retained by the abbey as a result of Brand's action, perhaps with the support of Ulf Topeson, another relative, in persuading King William to issue a writ allowing the abbot to retain the lands of his brothers and kinsmen which were held hereditarily and freely by the abbot.

Abbot Brand's Family

An account of Hereward's parentage which makes him the son of a Danish thegn who was the brother of Abbot Brand (or Brandr) of Peterborough and therefore member of a widespread Lincolnshire family certainly makes more sense than the more romantic accounts. Brand and his relatives were a band of kinsmen who acted in concert, endowing Peterborough, attesting one another's charters and helping each other out. Such kindred extended beyond siblings, spouses and parents to cousins, uncles and in-laws. The kindred held lands throughout Lincolnshire and across the Humber into Holderness. To identify Hereward's putative father, Brand's brothers must be identified. Abbot Brand had no less than four brothers; Asketil (also written Aschill, Askill, Eskill or Asketyl), Siric, Siworth and Godric. The three eldest have Danish names; the fourth and youngest, Godric, had an English name, implying that as youngest he was the 'baby' of the family and named by his mother, who was probably herself of an English family.

If they are considered in reverse order, youngest first, the likelihood of any of the younger brothers being Hereward's father can be reduced. Godric outlived all the others. He was a monk at Peterborough and in 1098, under William Rufus, he was elected by the other monks as the next abbot, after Turold. Rufus, as was his wont, demanded payment for recognition of the election. That was unfortunate. After Rufus' untimely death, Archbishop Anselm included Godric in the 'cleansing' of the Church and he was deposed on a charge of simony, that is, the purchase of office in the Church. As he had no choice but to pay Rufus and had not been a free agent it seems rather unfair, but a charge of simony was a useful way of removing abbots and bishops. It is likely that the real motive was to remove an 'English' monk to make way for a Norman. This story shows that Godric, chosen as abbot in 1096 or 1097, would have been far too young to be Hereward's father, as traditional accounts suggest that Hereward was eighteen years old in 1063 and so would have been born about 1045. Godric is likely to have been born around 1060, but there is no evidence as to the actual year.

Of the middle two, Siric and Siworth, little else is known, but entries in Domesday Book provide clues. Entries for North and South Muskham in Nottinghamshire reveal that these two estates were held by the baron Geoffrey Alselin, who was the Norman successor in all his lands of a certain Toki of Lincoln, for whom there are grounds for accepting that he was the father of the five brothers. In North Muskham land was held of Geoffrey Alselin by one 'Siward' (i.e. Siworth or Sigvatt) and in South Muskham by 'Seric' (i.e. Siric). There was also a Siric the Thegn with a small estate at West Keal, Lincolnshire. In Costock, Nottinghamshire, land was held by Saeric and his two brothers (who could be Siward and Godric). It cannot be proved that these men were Brand's brothers, but it is a significant coincidence that they had land once held by Toki. Also, curiously, a charter of Abbot Ailwin of Ramsey, issued during William Rufus' reign, is witnessed, among others, by *'Siward filius Toki'*. If these are the brothers, still holding lands in 1086 and after, then they too are too young to be likely candidates for Hereward's father. There is no clear evidence that the three younger brothers held large amounts of land before the Conquest, whereas Asketil, the king's thegn, did. He had much land in Lincolnshire and probably elsewhere and was rich enough to fit the description of 'one of the first in the land'. Eleventh-century writers, especially the scribes of Domesday Book, were fond of using contracted forms of personal names (known as hypochoristic contractions) and so this man's name is given variously in the sources as Aschill, Askill or Eskill.

So it would appear that Asketil (as he will be named from now on), probably the elder brother of Brand (as the eldest usually inherited most of the lands of the family), is the best candidate for Hereward's father. A king's thegn would certainly have been sufficiently influential to have secured his son's expulsion from the country.

Quite a lot is known about Asketil. The *Black Book of Peterborough*, containing the abbey's charters and other documents, describes Asketil as 'Tokisune', son of Toki. He held an estate at Manton on lease from his brother 'Brand the Monk', and, according to the 'Clamores' for the West Riding of Lincolnshire in Domesday Book, he held lands from King Edward 'and later', that is under Harold, at Scotter, Scotton and Raventhorpe (along with West Markham in Nottinghamshire, held by Godric in Domesday) '*in propria libertate*', that is literally 'in his own free possession', freely with the sake and soke. Most of these lands are found listed in Domesday Book as possessions of Peterborough Abbey, because the Abbot Brand had arranged to hold all of them in order to keep them out of the hands of lay Norman lords. Asketil held an estate at Walcote on Trent and at Barholme and Stowe as well as elsewhere, a total for Lincolnshire alone of some twenty-six carucates (the Danelaw equivalent of a hide, the unit of land taxation). For comparison, in Cambridgeshire several king's thegns held totals of land in the region of twenty-nine hides, twenty hides, or nineteen hides. Asketil is singled out in Domesday Book, in the Clamores; it insists that he was a king's thegn and never held his land under Maerleswein (the Sheriff of Lincolnshire) and that he held his several estates *'in propria libertate'*.

There is evidence of the transfer of lands to the abbey by Asketil. A charter, allegedly issued by King Edward and witnessed by Archbishop Cynsige of York who died in 1060, says that Asketil, King Edward's thegn, gave land at Walcote *'iuxta fluvium Humbrae'* to Abbot Leofric and Peterborough Abbey, when he was about to go to Rome on pilgrimage, on such terms that the abbey would have the land after his death and the lands of his brothers Siric and Siworth. It is considered of doubtful authenticity on the grounds that the clause about the 'pilgrimage' seems to have been borrowed from a similar clause in the next document on the same page, the Will of Leofgifu of London, though she died on her pilgrimage to Jerusalem. On the other hand, much of the information appears in the *Chronicle of Hugh Candidus*, which is earlier than the *Black Book*. It was quite common for English nobles to undertake the pilgrimage to Rome: Earl Tostig journeyed there and Cnut the Great went twice.

More interesting is the Charter of King Edward to Abbot Leofric, datable to 1060–1066 and witnessed by Lincolnshire thegns connected with Peterborough, and by Archbishop Ealdred of York who was given this see in 1060, confirming the agreement of Brand the monk to the lease of estates to his brother Asketil for a yearly rent. After his death, Scotton and Scotter were to revert to Peterborough, along with Thorpe (possibly Northorpe) instead of Manton (which was still held by the abbey in 1086).

The story told by this charter is that Brand gathered together the number of estates and then leased them to his brother Asketil, presumably in order to ensure that they came back to the abbey if Asketil died. Manton was acquired, by word of mouth, from his father, Toki; Scotton had been bought by Brand himself, and Scotter had been given to him by his brother Siric. The same information is found in Hugh Candidus, and records genuine transactions possibly during Harold's reign.

There is more to be said about Asketil. Ness Wapentake, in the Lincolnshire Clamores, states that Asketil was the king's thegn, and that he never held his land under Maerleswein (the Sheriff). Also, the shire testified that

> on the day on which King Edward was alive and dead and afterwards, Asketil had of King Edward these three manors, Scotton, Scotter, and 'Raventhorpe' (in Broughton which belonged to Maerleswein, hence the other entry) in his own jurisdiction.

In like manner he had North Muskham in Nottinghamshire, and he held one manor, Manton, of his brother Brand the monk in leasehold. Asketil is also recorded as having held land in Barholme and Stowe which was held in 1086 by Geoffrey of Cambrai. This is not the berewick attached to Witham-on-the-Hill and held by Turold's man Asfort. But it is significant that Asketil held land in the same locality, in Barholme Hundred near Witham-on-the-Hill, as did Hereward, of whom the Wapentake testified that he did not hold this berewick on the day he fled. The other brothers seem to have held their lands in northern Lincolnshire, north-west of Lincoln itself.

Asketil the king's thegn may have been much wealthier, and therefore far more important, than appears so far. He is the 'Askill Tokesune' who witnessed a charter of King Edward confirming Leofgifu of London's gift of Fiskerton to Peterborough Abbey, dated 1060. According to Walter of Whittlesey in his additions to Hugh Candidus' chronicle, Asketil *'filius Toke'* had about a dozen estates, including Walcote, North Muskham and Scotter. He then says of his list:

> This is what Brand the monk and afterwards Abbot, and Askil and Siric and Siworth, brothers, gave to God and St Peter and the brothers of Burgh.

There is a series of entries in other shires listing the lands of a king's thegn called Askill or Asketil of Ware, in Hertfordshire where he was succeeded by Ralph Taillebois; and an Aschil of Beckenham in Kent who was one of those with sake and soke in the shire, the mark of a king's thegn. As with other lands of Asketil of Ware, and Asketil Tokisune, the Kentish lands were later held by Odo of Bayeux who was one of those who benefited from the break-up of these large holdings. There is a difficulty in identifying Asketil of Ware with Asketil Tokesune arising from the simple fact that the Lincolnshire man is nowhere called 'of Ware' and no direct link can be made between estates in Lincolnshire and those in Bedfordshire, Hertfordshire and Northamptonshire. But it is certain that both were king's thegns and one of the marks of a king's thegn was that he could be referred to as 'of' a certain place, as for instance Eadric 'of Laxfield'. Lincolnshire is not one of the shires in which these expressions are used (except of five men named in the Clamores); instead, thegns are simply named and three are given the title 'Barn'. These are Arnketil, Siward (who was at Ely) and none other than Asketil. Some shires also identify king's thegns as 'a thegn of King Edward' (both Bedfordshire and Hertfordshire do so) but Lincolnshire does not. Asketil is said to have held his lands in Scotter, Scotton and Raventhorpe as 'of King Edward' but is not called 'a thegn of King Edward', although he certainly was one. Therefore, the fact that Asketil is not named as 'of Ware' nor called a thegn of King Edward, except indirectly, does not exclude the possibility that Asketil Tokesune and 'of Ware' are the same man.

This king's thegn of Ware, that is Asketil, held land in ten different places in Bedfordshire, but Ware, in Hertfordshire in 1086, was his main residence, rated at twenty-four hides and worth the considerable sum of £50 a year. In 1086 Hugh de Beauchamp held several estates as a result of 'the exchange of Ware'. The Hertfordshire entry for Ware says it belonged to Hugh de Grandmesnil. The Victoria County History for Hertfordshire, Vol. 1, provides in its introduction to the Domesday translation for that county the information that Eskil or Aschil is named as 'Anschil Waras' and as 'Aschi Wara' (fol. 133b), both representing the name Asketil of Ware, so that the king's thegn of Knebworth is Asketil of Ware. Furthermore, Hugh de Grandmesnil, by the 'exchange of Ware' with Ralph Taillebois (Tallegebosc) held the lands of Ralph's widow Azelina which were not included in her dowry, including an estate called Stotfold worth £30 in 1086, previously held by none other than 'Anschil of Ware', the thegn of King Edward.

Ware was a tremendous estate with land suitable for the use of thirty-eight ploughs and a population of over 100 men (their dependants were not counted), with five mills, a reserve for 400 eels, meadow and woodland, a park for wild beasts and, recently planted, a vineyard. For comparison, Ely, which counted as a town, was only assessed at ten hides and valued at £33, with land for twenty ploughs, a population of eighty-eight men (not counting the monks or the men's dependants), with meadow and pasture and a vineyard. Remarkably, its fishery produced 3,750 eels. Ware was surely developing into a town. The conclusion is that Asketil was a rich man. He seems to have held no other land in Hertfordshire, but several individuals were his commended men. He also had a sokeman at Westmill, and a thegn and one sokeman on his other estates. In Bedfordshire he had five other 'men', Almaer, Godwine and three sokemen. It seems unlikely (though not perhaps impossible, though there seems to be no other example of such a case) that there were two king's thegns called, to use the full form, Asketil, in which case it is possible that Asketil of Ware was Abbot Brand's brother, Asketil Tokisune, and so father of Hereward.

What of other lands belonging to Asketil? This thegn appears to have held relatively small pockets of land in twelve counties from Yorkshire in the north to Dorset in the south, and although it cannot be asserted that every one of these holdings is the land of this one man, there is no reason why most of them should not have been so held. That he was Asketil of Beckenham, holding with sake and soke, is quite possible. Thegns could certainly hold widely separated estates; for example Siward Barn from the Danelaw also had lands in Warwickshire; Maerleswein, Sheriff of Lincolnshire, held land in the south-west of England.

In Northamptonshire, Asketil is said to have held all of Earl Hugh's holdings and those of his men 'with sake and soke' totalling just over twenty-three hides. He is not called 'of Ware' nor given the title of king's thegn, but Earl Hugh is Hugh de Beauchamp, who later held so much of Asketil's land in Bedfordshire as well as lands received in the exchange of Ware. This connection seems to establish that Asketil in Northamptonshire was Asketil of Ware. If so, he was very wealthy indeed, holding over seventy-two carucates in the Danelaw and over fifty-eight hides in the rest of the country, possibly even sixty-five. No wonder men later thought that Hereward had to be an earl's son.

Asketil's land at Colmworth in Bedfordshire held the 'soke' of the manor of Easton in Huntingdonshire held

by 'men' of Asketil, which shows that he held land in
Huntingdonshire. The text of Domesday also states
firmly that this Asketil was 'the predecessor of Hugh
de Beauchamp', which confirms that he is Asketil of
Ware. Most of the lands attributed to 'Asketil' in all
these counties had been given to a number of different
Norman successors. In Hertfordshire, Bedfordshire
and Northamptonshire, his successor was Hugh de
Beauchamp, and in Lincolnshire much of it was saved
from direct Norman occupation by Abbot Brand, though
several of his holdings went to Odo of Bayeux, who also
held the Kentish lands attributed to Asketil and one
estate in Surrey.

It is difficult to say that these estates all belonged to
the same man. Most of these estates are quite small and
well detached from the major holdings. Where the larger
sets of estates are concerned, it looks as though King
William had decided not to allow such a great 'Honour'
to be held by one man, as that might make the holder
far too strong for comfort.

The connection between Asketil and Hereward lies in
the claim that Abbot Brand was Hereward's uncle and
the fact that Hereward held lands which became part
of the inheritance of Brand's family which passed into
the possession of Peterborough Abbey. If these points
are accepted, then Asketil, the king's thegn and probably
the eldest of the brothers, is the most likely candidate
for the role of Hereward's father. Accepting this, it then
appears that the father of these five brothers was called
Toki. Can he be further identified? He is not likely to
have been a nobody.

Toki of Lincoln

The story surrounding the lease of lands by Brand to
Asketil claims that some of the land was a gift to Brand

from Toki, who therefore must have had land to spare. Much of the land associated with Asketil, centring on Scotter, lies near Lincoln, somewhat to the north. The most prominent person in Lincoln was a rich burgess, as he would have been called by the mid-twelfth century, called Toki of Lincoln and also known as Toki son of Auti (or Outi). Auti himself was one of the moneyers of Lincoln, which would account for the foundation of the family's wealth. Toki was one of those who had 'sake and soke and toll and team' in Lincolnshire and other counties and had some sixty 'messuages', that is houses with land attached to them. He owned his own hall (which was free of all customary dues) and two-and-a-half churches. Over thirty of his messuages he had rights of letting and from each received one penny as 'landgable', a rent. His hall and thirty messuages, and all his other lands in six counties, eventually passed to Geoffrey Alselin, while the other thirty were seized, not exactly legally, by Remigius, Bishop of Lincoln, upon the site of which he built his cathedral. Toki also had sake and soke in Northamptonshire, Nottinghamshire and Yorkshire and sokes in Ruskington, Laxton and Kesteven. He is probably not the Toki listed in Cambridgeshire, as that Toki's lands did not go to Geoffrey Alselin.

Sokes were complex estates centred on a main village, with dependent pieces of property called berewicks or sokelands, which might be whole villages or just parts of a village. The sokemen living there owed suit of court in the head village and paid a money rent. The customary dues, especially geld, were paid to the king through the holder of the soke. Thus Toki of Lincoln makes a convincing father for the wealthy king's thegn and an Abbot of Peterborough. Toki's father was Auti, the Lincoln moneyer of that name, and one of his estates at Ashby de la Launde was held in conjunction with Asketil. He had a moderate holding, some eight hides

worth £8 and about thirty carucates worth £25. One
other possible connection is that Toki was the owner of
a large number of houses in Lincoln, his messuages, and
Domesday says that Asketil held six carucates in Scotton
and adds:

> In Lincoln are three burgesses rendering (to Asketil's
> manor of Scotton) five shillings and he has fifty acres of
> meadow and thirty-six acres of scrubland.

It looks as though Asketil owned property in his father's
home city of Lincoln.

The Rest of the Clan

Abbot Brand is also credited with a number of other
prominent relatives, especially the brothers Ulf and
Haelfdan, sons of Tope. Tope must have died sometime
before 1066, as only one piece of land is listed for him,
at Kirmington, Lincolnshire. Ulf Topeson is found as a
witness to the writ by which King William confirmed
Brand and his abbey in possession of all the lands held as
the gifts of Brand, his kinsmen and relatives, by the 'good
men' who interceded with the king on Brand's behalf
when he committed the faux pas of seeking confirmation
of his election as abbot from Edgar the Aetheling rather
than from the as yet uncrowned William. Ulf's wife
was called Madselin, as is known from their will, and
his mother may have been called Aedeva (which might
explain where that name came from in 'Ingulf'). His land
holding in Lincolnshire must be carefully distinguished
from that of another prominent Lincolnshire thegn called
Ulf 'Fenisc' or the Fenman. It was Ulf 'Fenisc' who was
one of those with sake and soke in the shire and his
successor was Gilbert de Ghent, whereas Ulf Topeson
was replaced by Drogo de la Bevrière. It can be estimated

that Ulf Topeson had some eighty-five or more carucates worth about £60.

That Ulf and Haelfdan were brothers and sons of Tope is certain: both have the appellation 'Tope' or 'Topesune' added to their name. It is also clear that Ulf lost his lands, after or at the same time as Hereward's rebellion in Ely, to his successor Drogo de la Bevrière. It is less easy to establish what their relationship to Brand was. But the actions of Brand in assisting Haelfdan after he had lost his Lincolnshire lands, about fourteen carucates, are those of a kinsman. The lands had fallen into the hands of Bishop Remigius, who had also taken the thirty messuages in Lincoln belonging to Toki. Hugh Candidus says bluntly that the abbey lost possession of Dunsby, leased by Brand to his kinsman Haelfdan

> because King William had taken all of Haelfdan's land from him and given it to Remigius, Bishop of Lincoln, and so Remigius himself unjustly took away Dunsby from St Peter's.

Much of Haelfdan's land as recorded in Domesday was held by Bishop Remigius. Haelfdan's total pre-Conquest holding had been in the region of twenty-two hides worth about £15 and 127 carucates worth £87.

In the *Gesta Herewardi*, Hereward is said to have several relatives, and Gaimar confirms this. Only a few are partially identifiable. These seem to be his cousins Siward the Red (Rufus) and Siward the White (Albus), although their parentage is not known. They could be sons of either Ulf or Haelfdan. Another possible relative may be Rolf or Rothulfr, holding lands in Domesday which are said, in the *Brevi Cartula* of Peterborough Abbey, to have been given to the abbey by Asketil. On the other hand, he may only be a tenant or 'man' of Asketil. There is also Alnoth. His land passed to the Bishop of

Durham, at Mavis Enderby, and East Keal. He shared
the eight carucates at Scotter with Asketil. Domesday
amalgamates their two manors into one. Another possible
relative is 'Elfsi' (from Aelfsige perhaps), identified in
the Peterborough *Black Book* and in Hugh Candidus
as '*Elfsi Infans filius Outi*' or '*Elfsi Cild filius Outi*' (i.e.
Auti) who gave Turlebi to the abbey, that is Thurlby near
Bourne. The descendants of Auti the moneyer do seem
to have been numerous.

4

Hereward the Outlaw and Exile

A Soldier of Fortune

There are several quite sound reasons for accepting that Hereward was sent or driven into exile in 1063, probably in the autumn. Domesday Book states, in connection with Hereward's loss of his land at Rippingale, taken on an annual lease from Abbot Ulfcytel of Crowland and forfeit for non-compliance with the terms, that he had lost the land before he 'fled the country'. The survey also refers to Barholme and says that Hereward did not have it 'on the day he fled'. Both references are best understood as referring to pre-Conquest events as they are concerned to establish who were the 'antecessores', that is predecessors, of the new Norman owners.

Dating the Exile

'Ingulf' (*History of Crowland Abbey*) places the appointment of Ulfcytel in 1052 but, after reporting Wulfstan II's consecration as Bishop of Worcester in 1062 (probably in August), says that Ulfcytel now began building the new church. Other sources indicate that Crowland was, in King Edward's reign, in common with several other monasteries, held by Abbot Leofric of Peterborough, certainly until about 1062. Leofric had been given charge of a number of monasteries which were then administered as a group, so reducing the abbots effectively to the status of priors, and this looks like an attempt to follow the Cluniac pattern of monastic administration. This gave him central control over the various houses.

Perhaps King Edward had the idea of putting a group of monasteries under one abbot who would supervise them all. These were not daughter houses but autonomous monasteries each with its own abbot who was under Leofric's governance. The abbot certainly had some sort of monastic hegemony over several monasteries: Abingdon, Crowland, Ely and Thorney as well as Peterborough itself. As for Crowland, there the abbots were appointed by King Edward at the will of Leofric of Peterborough and this may have applied elsewhere. The *Peterborough Chronicle* records that Leofric made Peterborough a rich foundation in his time, as it became known as the 'Golden Borough' which 'waxed greatly in land and gold and silver'. It also asserts that King Edward gave to

> St Peter and to him (Leofric) the abbacy at Barton and that at Coventry which earl Leofric who was his uncle had before made, and that at Crowland and that at Thorney.

The experiment seems to have been ended in 1062 and Ulfcytel was making the most of his independence by commencing a building programme. He might also have decided at that time that Crowland needed a protector or advocate, and attempted to recruit Hereward in that role because he was already performing a similar service for Peterborough. Unfortunately, Hereward did not keep to his side of the bargain and shortly afterwards was exiled. According to the *Gesta*, Hereward was exiled, at his father's insistence, because he 'stirred up sedition among the populace and tumult among the ordinary people'. Was he involved in the events of 1062–63? He was then said to be eighteen years old, quite old enough to fight. The *Gesta* account sends Hereward on a series of romantic, even fabulous, adventures in Ireland, Cornwall and Northumbria which are the stuff of medieval romance. After these putative adventures he ends up in Flanders, and what happened to him there is an entirely different matter.

Exile

In fact, what seems to confirm a pre-Conquest date for Hereward's exile, to support the claims of the *Gesta Herewardi*, is the remarkable extent to which the persons he encountered during his exile in Flanders can be shown to be exactly the sort of people he could have been expected to meet and, not only that, but the war in which he is said to have taken part can even be identified. The account given in the *Gesta* supports, from an opposing point of view, the events of that war. It is thus possible to reveal the outlines of his military career on the continent and so explain why he proved such a formidable foe for King William.

The *Gesta* events fall into two distinct sections. The first section (derived it would seem from the fragments of Leofric the Deacon's book which fell into the hands of the anonymous writer of the *Gesta* in the form of 'a few scattered leaves partly rotted by damp and decayed' or torn, of which the author says it was his intention to note down in English 'the acts of giants and warriors from the fables of old') draws attention to the fictitious aspects of the work. The second section makes use of an account of the siege of Ely closely paralleled by the account in the *Liber Eliensis* attributed to the monk Richard of Ely.

There is also Gaimar's work which, in the section concerning Hereward, begins by talking about King Arthur and Mordred and other Arthurian characters and then launches into the story of Haveloc the Dane, before relating his own version of the history of England from 565 to 1071, which concludes with his account of the siege of Ely followed by the death of Hereward. The work follows the accounts in a version of the *Anglo-Saxon Chronicle* not now extant but this is used as a frame for a series of anecdotes about the various kings and nobles mentioned derived from 'the good book of Oxford which Walter the Deacon made', that is from Geoffrey of Monmouth, with additions by Gaimar himself. In fact, he says that he writes verses 'concerning the most noble deeds' and includes the rural entertainments, the amusements and the conversation of the feasts held by King Henry I. He even says that his work began with the story of Troy (just like Monmouth) and that of Jason and the Golden Fleece. It is essential to remember that this fashionable mixture in twelfth-century works of fact and fiction was expected and accepted by audiences of that time. The *Gesta Herewardi* follows this fashion.

Although it contains much that rings true, especially in its account of the siege of Ely, a version of which is in the *Liber Eliensis*, it also contains the far more romantic material derived from Leofric the Deacon's little book of fables. Although some would insist that it is impossible to distinguish all of this material from the more reliable statements, an attempt to do so can be made by applying a certain amount of common sense. While much of the introductory material, including what is said about Hereward's background and parentage and his adventures in Northumbria, Cornwall and Ireland, can be seen as included for its entertainment value, the major part of the body of the work is written in a far less fabulous style and can be verified from other sources and, allowing for the author's tenuous grip on chronology, can be reordered into a narrative which provides at least an outline of Hereward's real exploits.

Hereward's background and parentage have been discussed in Chapter Two, so it is now time to look briefly at the matter concerning his exile in Ireland, Cornwall and Northumbria. The tale about his adventures in Ireland and Cornwall is similar in content to the story of Tristan and Isolde and other romantic tales. Hereward is the mysterious stranger who helps the King of Cornwall's daughter escape the clutches of a man she does not love in order to marry the King of Ireland's son. However, there can have been no 'King of Cornwall' in the England of Edward the Confessor and therefore no 'princess' to fall for a King of Ireland's son. As Domesday Book shows, land in Cornwall was largely in the hands of the Godwinson family and their supporters. In 1086 King William held twelve estates described as having been the property of Harold. Almost the whole of the rest of Cornwall was held by the Count of Mortain and he holds estates which formerly belonged to Queen Edith, Gytha (wife of Earl Godwin) and Wulfnoth, who might be the youngest Godwinson. Other lands were held by various prominent men such as Ralf Staller, Maerleswein and Esgar (also a staller), or major thegns like Beorhtric. There was no room for what Kingsley in his novel called 'petty kinglets'. As for Northumbria, it is there that Hereward allegedly encountered Gilbert of Ghent, who, without a shred of evidence, is asserted to be Hereward's godfather, and had invited him to come north. There Hereward had his famous fight with a bear, causing 'women and girls to sing about him in their dances' and is offered knighthood by Gilbert. Others, envious of the offer made to Hereward, attempt unsuccessfully to kill him.

There is no evidence that Gilbert I of Ghent owned property in England. He is not mentioned as one of those who fought at Hastings or in the earliest campaigns, but his wealth and huge grants of land held in 1086 suggest that he at least sent a large contingent of knights to support the Conqueror. He is not mentioned until 1069 when he was a member of the force occupying York. It is therefore far more likely that Hereward first met him in Flanders.

Gilbert was the younger son of Ralph of Alost, hereditary 'advocate' (protector) of St Peter's, Ghent, and through his mother, Gisela, was first cousin once removed of King William's wife Matilda. His eldest brother was Baldwin I of Ghent. Gilbert moved in the circles in which the *Gesta* says Hereward also moved. Why the author of the *Gesta* linked him to Hereward in Northumbria is a mystery, and probably only a simple error of chronology. A more likely explanation is that the two met in Flanders and that it was then that Gilbert could have offered Hereward knighthood. Hereward returned to England before Abbot Brand's death in 1069, so they might well have come into contact during the northern rebellions. When he is first mentioned, in connection with the attack on Peterborough, Hereward is already a well-known outlaw who needed no further introduction.

The fight with a half-human bear looks like pure fiction, although there is evidence from the chronicles of the counts of Ardres and Guines of bears being imported from England specifically for use in bear-fighting. On the other hand, there is the legend that Earl Siward of Northumbria was supposed to be the offspring of a woman and a bear, arising no doubt from his strength, hairiness and warlike abilities. It might be that Hereward fought a similarly endowed warrior. But he could equally have met and slain an escaped bear.

Flanders

The main location of Hereward's exploits in exile was Flanders and here the matter is very different. As Elisabeth Van Houts (*Hereward and Flanders*, Anglo-Saxon England No. 28, 1999, from which most of what is said here about Hereward is derived) has shown, almost all of the notables encountered by Hereward in Flanders, as well as the places he visited and the battles in which he took part, can be verified; they are real people, places and events and it is by no means impossible that Hereward played quite a prominent role. The *Gesta* says that Hereward became a soldier under the Count of Flanders in his wars with the Count of Guines, coming up against the latter's '*nepos*' called Hoibrict. Hereward is said to have been shipwrecked near St Omer, where he met a wealthy lady called Turfrida who was being wooed in marriage by the '*nepos*' of the lord of St Valéry. He is described as travelling around with other warriors, taking part in 'military contests' (which are most likely early tournaments) at Bruges and Poitiers, and comes to excel as a fighting man and instructor of younger soldiers. During this time he defeats Hoibrict and impresses Turfrida, who falls for him. His paternal cousins, Siward the Blond (or White) and Siward the Red, join him in Flanders, and Hereward kills several enemies.

Hereward then joins a military expedition to 'Scaldemariland' (led by the Count's son Robert) in his capacity as 'Magister Militum' [leader of the soldiers or master of the knights], its purpose being to enforce the payment of tribute to Flanders by the people of that region. Before peace was signed, Hereward bought two fine horses, Swallow and Lightfoot, and returned to Flanders to find that the old Count had died and his successor had not yet taken his place. Hereward and

Martin Lightfoot, his servant, return briefly to England, leaving the two Siwards to protect Turfrida, now called his wife.

Of this lady, Turfrida, little can be established. Her name is Gallo-German rather than a corruption of an English form like Thorfrith, but her parents are unknown. She is said by the *Gesta* to have come from a wealthy family, to be learned and to be skilled in needlework. Her family was rich and prominent enough for her to have attracted as a potential suitor a *nepos* (grandson or nephew) of the Lord of St Valéry, that is probably St Valéry-sur-Somme, King William's embarkation port. That lord cannot at present be identified because of confusion with another family who took their name and title from St Valéry-en-Caux in Normandy. Turfrida does not appear to have belonged to the de Warenne circle; if she had, the *Gesta* or the *Hyde Chronicle* would have made something of it. It has been suggested that she might have been the daughter of Wulfric Rabel the Castellan of St Omer, but evidence is lacking. She is described as beautiful, rich and skilled in magical and liberal arts and as having the sagacity of a man when confronted by danger. Her advice was invaluable to Hereward, says the *Gesta Herewardi*, and he sorely missed it after they parted. That Hereward should have married a daughter of a commander under whom he served fits the known pattern of soldiers of fortune contracting marriage with the heiress of their commanders.

In between times, while based in Flanders, Hereward had returned to England and discovered that his homeland was now 'subject to the rule of foreigners' and almost ruined by their exactions. Hereward drove out the French occupants of his home and took revenge for the death of his younger brother, was knighted by Abbot Brand and his companions were similarly knighted by Wulfwine of Ely. Other activities involved the slaying of

William de Warenne's 'brother' Frederick (actually his brother-in-law). A short period in Flanders followed in which he rejoined his wife Turfrida and was asked to fight for Baldwin, 'a most famous soldier [knight] of that province' against the lord of Picquigny aided by the lord of Brabant. After that Hereward returned to England, accompanied by his wife and cousins, and took up his struggle against the Normans, as recorded elsewhere.

His Career Begins

Where does all this fit into what is known of Flemish history between 1063 and 1070? Firstly, there is the arrival by shipwreck in the County of Guines, on the Flanders coast near the estuary of the River Aa which led straight to St Omer. Here he met Manasses the Old, that is Count Manasses I of Guines who flourished in the mid-eleventh century. The Counts of Guines were responsible for dealing with shipwrecks on that coast, which explains why Hereward was taken first to Manasses. This dates his arrival in Flanders to 1064–65. He then goes to 'St Bertin', that is the abbey in St Omer. The *Gesta* places Hereward's activities in western Flanders, especially at Bruges and further south at Poitiers, where he takes part in military competitions, that is, shows or tournaments. Such shows are usually dated as having been begun in the late eleventh century. The earliest known reference, other than in the *Gesta*, is a description from Valenciennes in 1114, and it is certain that this period saw the beginning of such events.

There is plenty of evidence for military activity in the Cambrai–Valenciennes area in the 1060s and 1070s which would have attracted the participation of mercenaries and soldiers of fortune. Hereward might well have been taken into the service of the Bishop of Cambrai, Lietbert. There is an interesting clue in the foundation charter of the monastery of St Sepulchre, datable to early 1065. The building was part of the Bishop's aim to enlarge the city and use the new monastery as part of a fortification on the south side of the town. It was deliberately placed behind the town battlements and ditch. This was essential because of the warfare then going on between the bishop, who was also Count of Cambrai, and the Castellans John of Arras and Hugh, as well as a constant threat of a takeover by the Counts of Flanders. The bishop would have needed soldiers, and proceeded to surround himself with mercenaries.

Was Hereward one of them? A charter of 1065 was witnessed, among others, by nine '*milites*' (soldiers or knights), and one of these was the '*miles Herivvardi*'. Was this indeed Hereward (*Hereuuardus* in English sources)? Herivvard is a Germanic name, known in eastern France, but no other person is so named in any Flemish or northern French source. The time, 1065, and place, Cambrai, could be right and as the story of Hereward's arrival shows, he was in the area. He might well have chosen to serve the bishop for a time before moving on. This would also explain the tale in the *Gesta* of his having given assistance to a very famous Baldwin. This was perhaps Baldwin II of Hainault, a son of Baldwin VI of Flanders who was also Count of Hainault, 1051–1070. His opponent was Arnulf, the '*vidame*' (vicomte) or Lord of Picquigny. These '*vidames*' of Picquigny were hereditary officers of the Bishops of Amiens. The lord of Brabant was also present, that is Henry II, 1063–1079, of Brabant and Louvain. The area of conflict was south-west of Cambrai. So considering the bishop's need for men who could give him expert military advice and Hereward's known presence in that region, it is surely logical to suggest that the charter witness and Hereward the Exile were the same man.

St Omer

The only place which figures prominently in the *Gesta*, other than Scaldemariland, is St Omer. This town had long-established and strong ties with England. The information from the extant sources derives from the monastery of St Bertin. A writer of saints' lives, Goscelin, came from there, before becoming a wandering scholar in England for the next fifty years (1058–1108). The monk Folcard also came to England, some time between 1050 and 1069, and became abbot of Thorney in the Fens until deposed by Lanfranc in 1085, along with Ulfcytel of Crowland. These two men are the link between St Bertin at St Omer and the Fenland monasteries of Thorney, Peterborough, Ramsey and Ely, which perhaps explains the transmission to England of the tales of Hereward in Flanders.

But the secular ties are equally strong. In 1065, Count Baldwin V gave shelter there to Earl Tostig and his wife, Baldwin's half-sister Judith, making Tostig deputy commander with a house and land (*Vita Edwardi* p. 55) and so either alongside or superior to Wulfric Rabel the Castellan. Possibly Hereward was attracted to St Omer by the hope of taking service with an English rather than a Flemish lord or even the chance of a return to England with Tostig, who still harboured such dreams. Hereward seems to have remained at St Omer until he enlisted in the service of Robert the Frisian. It might well be that it was at St Omer that Hereward encountered two men who also figure in his history. The first, as has been described, was Gilbert of Ghent, and the other, Frederick of Oosterzele-Scheldewindeke, the brother-in-law of William de Warenne who had married Frederick's sister.

Frederick's family were the hereditary advocates of St Bertin at St Omer, which explains where he and Hereward might have first met and in such a meeting probably can be found the reasons for Hereward's assassination of Frederick. This is reported not only by the *Gesta* but also by the early twelfth-century work the *Hyde Chronicle* (part of the *Liber de Hyda*) which comes from the de Warenne circle in East Anglia. This work knows nothing of Hereward's sojourn in Flanders, and calls Frederick the brother rather than brother-in-law of de Warenne, but is well informed about the de Warenne links with Flanders. William de Warenne inherited Frederick's English lands after his killing, while he, William, and his sons retained the advocacy of St Bertin until about the 1090s. Frederick's brother Gerbod was for a time King William's first Earl of Chester, until he was called back to Flanders in 1071. Frederick might well have come to England with him, there to be assassinated by the vengeful Hereward.

English sources maintain that Turfrida, whom Hereward married after making his fortune in Scaldemariland, was divorced by him after 1071 because he wished to marry the '*uxor*' (wife or widow) of 'Earl' Dolfin, called Aelfthryth (Alftruda) by Gaimar. It is possible that Dolfin was one of the three sons of Cospatrick I, Earl of Dunbar. The youngest son, Cospatrick II, eventually succeeded his father, and the middle son Waltheof became a monk at Crowland (and abbot 1126–38). The latter fact might explain where the story originated, although Ingulf knows nothing of it. Nothing is known for certain about the eldest son other than his name, Dolfin, and that he was expelled from Cumbria in 1092 by William Rufus. The curious thing is that Cospatrick II was never referred to as earl, only as the 'brother of Dolfin'. It may be that he was regarded as keeping the earldom available for his missing elder brother. Nothing is known of a marriage for Dolfin, though eldest sons were expected to marry. If he was the Dolfin named in the *Gesta*, it might be that he was in some way incapable of undertaking his role as earl, perhaps disabled or unable to consummate his marriage or even imprisoned by some enemy for life. These can only remain conjectures, but if some such fate had befallen him, his wife, if she was Aelfthryth, might well have left him for Hereward.

Scaldemariland

Consideration has been given to most of the evidence which suggests that the *Gesta*'s account of Hereward's exile in Flanders is based on fact. It remains to investigate the most compelling part of the story, which is also the most firmly grounded aspect of his activities. According to the *Gesta Herewardi*, Hereward took service with 'Robert, the Count's son' as Magister Militum, that is commander (in this context) of the mercenary troops, for an expedition into Scaldemariland in order to compel the people there to pay tribute money. The army travelled in forty ships to enforce the count's demand for the payment which he claimed had been withheld for a long time. As the *Gesta Herewardi* has it:

> The Count of Flanders had sent officers into Frisia to secure taxes which had long been withheld and to make a valuation of the territory. This became an opportunity to send Hereward into that province with an army under the Prince's own general.

Fighting ensued and there was something of a stalemate, as was often the case in medieval battles.

Robert the Count's son then launched a more determined second attack and found that the whole area had risen against him and he was attacked 'from all sides from the island and the sea', by those seeking to ravage the Flemish borders and drive out the count. The men of the area feared that they might become subject to foreigners 'like the English people to the French' (which dates this to 1066–67). Hereward suggested setting fire to the chariots and wagons of the enemy and even threatened to burn their ambassadors. He led a force of 300 men ahead of the main army and they wreaked great slaughter. Hereward drew up a battle line on high ground and with 1,000 cavalry and 600 armed men he attacked and killed those guarding the enemy camp by striking from the rear. This was all quite typical of medieval warfare in which 'victory' went to the side which had the nerve to stay longest on the battlefield.

The people of Scaldemariland sought a truce and to negotiate a renewal of ancient treaties and their confirmation. The count insisted that the tribute be doubled. Meanwhile Hereward, as commander of the mercenaries, suggested that his men share out among themselves everything that they had acquired in Scaldemariland, an action which was later brought up by William de Warenne as a reason for his especial hostility towards Hereward. That is the *Gesta*'s version.

As Elisabeth Van Houts has deduced, in the *Vita S. Willibrordi* of Abbot Thiofrid of Echternach (*c.* 1081 to after 1105) there is an account of what must be the same expedition from the opposing point of view. Echternach held land on the island of Walcheren, one of the islands of the Scheldt estuary, and the life of the saint contains the story of the attempt by a younger son of Count Baldwin to extract unpaid taxes from the unwilling inhabitants of the islands. He is said to have led a force of French- and German-speaking troops, i.e. mercenaries, by land and sea across the Scaldemermur. In the ensuing struggle the invaders were driven back with heavy casualties and only three islanders were killed. The victors then sent two captured banners, taken from the Flemish army, back to Echternach as thanks to the saint for his support. However, dissension then broke out among the islanders and Abbot Thiofrid intervened as peacemaker to negotiate a settlement.

These accounts, from the *Gesta* and the *Vita*, conflict; they were after all written for different purposes and come from the opposing sides. The *Gesta Herewardi* is magnifying the deeds of its protagonist, Hereward, and Echternach is defending its right to its property against the rapacious Flemings. But both identify the leader of the expedition as Robert, younger son of the Count of Flanders, which must be Robert 'the Frisian', Baldwin V's second son and count himself from 1071 to 1093. He is known to have sought to extend his authority over the border lands between Flanders and Holland (1063–1071).

Both accounts use the same name for the target of the expedition, a good reason for believing that they are talking about the same events. The names 'Scaldemermur' and 'Scaldemariensis' occur only in the *Vita* and the *Gesta* and no other eleventh- or twelfth-century works, but they do occur in later medieval records where they are applied to islands in the estuary of the Scheldt in the province of Zeeland. The northern and southern borders of the island area are called respectively 'Scoudemarediep' and 'Scaldemermur'. The latter name is a compound of Scalde=Scheldt and Mere=sea water or lake in Old Dutch. A related form was Scaldemare (land) as applied to islands on the southern edge of the area. The *Vita* says that Walcheren, where Echternach held property, lay across the Scaldemermur, and mentions also the town of Middelburg. The *Gesta* gives no details except to mention sand dunes (which are found near Walcheren) and the '*Castra Scaldemariensium*', which may be the fortifications of Middelburg, Domburg and Souburg. Both accounts tell of the use of ships during the attacks.

The *Gesta* insists that the inhabitants agreed to pay double the tax they previously paid as part of a new settlement rather than pay what was paid in their father's time. Nothing is now known about what these taxes were but the whole area had been given to the Count of Flanders in 1012 by King Henry II and confirmed in 1056 by Agnes, widow of Henry III, on behalf of her son Henry IV. Some sort of renegotiation of the taxes had almost occurred, and Robert's efforts were the result of a refusal to pay on the part of the islanders. Robert celebrated Whitsun 1067 with his parents, surely marking his return. The whole affair fits nicely into what is known of the rivalries of the various princes of lands around the Scheldt Estuary.

Other sources are of little help. The Annals of St Bertin say that in 1063 Robert 'surreptitiously entered Frisia' and Lambert of Hersfeld says Robert was twice beaten back during expeditions to Frisia before he became count. The *Gesta* account suggests a plausible date for all this. The end is definitely verifiable. The *Gesta* says that the Flemings retired from the fray when news came of Baldwin V's death, and that occurred on 1 September 1067, at a time when Baldwin VI was busy in either Hainault or Ponthieu. That puts the whole expedition in the summer of 1067, with Hereward's return to England probably in the autumn of the same year. This also explains his absence from the battles of Stamford Bridge and Hastings. On a minor point; Hereward is said to have bought two fine horses before he left, and it is known that they were available on the islands, especially Walcheren, as Drogo of St Winnocsbergen confirms in his translation of St Lewinna (written 1058–68). There seems to be no real room for doubt about where Hereward was between 1063 and 1067, nor about where he gained the experience to oppose King William at Ely.

5

The Isle of Ely in the Eleventh Century

No account of the warfare around Ely can be constructed without first considering the topography and geography of the Isle as it was in the eleventh century. The accounts in the sources provide enigmatic and contradictory clues to the environment within which the fighting took place. There is the contradiction between the idyllic pastoral paradise described by the knight 'Deda' and the picture of a desolate, waterlogged hell full of stagnant pools and deadly bogs. The higher ground is described as wooded, even as part of the 'Brunneswald', yet surrounded by great meres and marshes cutting the Isle off from what can realistically be described as the mainland, protecting it from attack. The great Fens defended the Isle.

There were several different types of Fen. Some was reed swamp and other parts sedge. On the higher ground or Fen Carr grew alders and other woodland, while the rest was either open water or bog so that the area around the solid ground of the Isle was indeed waterlogged and marshy. The water table was probably anything up to 30 feet higher than it is today, bringing the marsh well up towards what is now Broad Street in Ely. Only after the Ely Ouse changed its course, probably in the thirteenth century, did the town spread down towards the river on the eastern side, resulting in the construction of the hythes, wharves and boatyards. Differing sections of the community in the twelfth century had their own hythe or landing place; the monastery was served by the 'Monks' Hythe'; townsfolk by 'Broad Hythe'; those bringing cattle to market by 'Stock Hythe' and the Castlemen by 'Castle Hythe'.

To the north, the Wash, in the eleventh century, extended south of its present shoreline, funnelling down to Wisbech, and into it flowed the ancient courses of the Lark, the Cam and the Little Ouse forming the 'Old Wellenhee' or Wellstream, joined upstream by the Nene and the Western Ouse. To the north-west the Fens extended as far as Lincoln, bypassing Rippingale and Bourne which lay on its westernmost margin. In the Fens, extinct rivers and watercourses can be detected from the presence of 'roddons' (also called by some rodhams). These are banks of sand or silt set above the level of the Fens as a result of the shrinkage of the peat and they are the natural levees of tidal rivers.

Vast areas of the original Fenland were once totally untamed marsh and fen consisting of deep pools, sheets of open water, and copses of alder and willow. Through it ran streams and rivers among reed beds and stands of rush and sedge. It abounded in wildlife; and all who went there were exposed to the often unwelcome attentions of those who had chosen a wild life.

The whole of the Fenlands surrounding Ely were composed not only of these great meres and marshes but also of a multitude of streams and rivers, fed by the River Great Ouse and by the Cam, then referred to as '*Gronta fluminis*' or River Granta. As much of the terrain was at or well below sea-level, these streams and rivers meandered through the marshes, often changing their course as a result of floods arising from heavy rainfall or inundations from the sea. The normal access to the

Isle, and of course the monastery, as well as to the farms and villages of the Isle, was by water. Such causeways as there were stopped short at the rivers (and resumed their way beyond them), which might be crossed by ferries but rarely by bridges before the twelfth century. This explains the frequency with which names ending in '-eth' for hythe are found, not just Aldreth (the alor-hythe or landing stage of the Alders) but, for example, Shepreth, Meldreth and even Earith. Only in the twelfth century does the *Chronicle of Ramsey Abbey* (1178) record that the chief entrance to the Isle was the causeway built by King William, but without saying exactly where it was. In an extended passage, the *Liber Eliensis* agrees. It says that the Isle was never cut off from the sea but that access to it, from the landward approaches, was prevented by the meres and marshes. It adds that it

> used to be reached by boat but because it was dangerous for boats to go there, a causeway has now been made through the marshy sedge-bank and it is possible to go there on foot.

The *Gesta Stephani* in Stephen's reign states, when discussing that king's attack on Ely, then held by the rebel Bishop Nigel, by means of a pontoon bridge at Aldreth, that Ely was still

> impenetrably surrounded on all sides by meres and fens, accessible only in one place where a very narrow track affords the scantiest of entries.

The final proof that King William built at least one causeway comes from his own hand. There is a writ, Regesta No. 155, dated to 1082 and addressed to Archbishop Lanfranc, the Count of Mortain and Bishop Geoffrey of Coutances (commanding an inquiry into Ely lands so that they can be restored to its demesne), which has a most interesting ending. It reads:

> Lastly, those men are to maintain the causeway at Ely who by the King's command have done so hitherto.

But all these references to a causeway and possibly to the approach by way of Aldreth as well as to a bridge at Aldreth, probably the work of King William and later taken over and strengthened by Bishop Hervey (who was not satisfied that the locals were maintaining it properly), are to works which only came into existence after King William had captured the Isle and do not mean that there was a useable way on to the Isle earlier in the eleventh century.

The Isle

The Isle was truly an island (indeed, almost two as, had the waters broken through above Stretham, the northern part would have been divided from the southern part). Eventually, three major causeways led to the Isle, one from Soham via Stuntney, another from Earith, and a third from Willingham via Belsar's Hill (an Iron Age structure used by the Romans in their day; the name means *Bel Assis* or Fair Seat) to Aldreth; this was the ancient track called the Mare's Way, or meres way. It was narrow and winding and waterlogged and unsuitable for war horses. But at the end of these causeways there were no bridges; the land was too unstable to support a permanent structure. These three causeways were made after the Norman settlement. Belsar's Hill today is still an impressive circular earthwork with a rampart and ditch. The rampart is 6.3 metres wide and 2.1 metres high in places and the ditch is 8 metres wide. It encloses an area 240 metres in diameter. It was once thought to be Norman work from the time of the siege of Ely but is in fact from the Iron Age. However, it was probably utilised as a convenient, ready-made defensible ring-work by King William's men and it may lie behind reports of a small castle (*castellulum*) at Aldreth.

The shape of the Isle enters the picture also. The abbey and the town of Ely stood on a large semi-island, stretching from Downham-in-the-Isle in the north as far as Stretham to the south, running in a rough west-facing semi-circle around a great bay in which Coveney stood out above the waters, 'Cofa's Island in the bay', and beyond that Wardy Hill, 'the Isle from which watch was kept' towards the 'March' or boundary between Eastern and Middle Anglia. That there was a town as claimed by the text of the *Anglo-Saxon Chronicle* for 1036, recording the death at Ely of the Aetheling Alfred, brother of Edward the Confessor, has now been confirmed by the Cambridgeshire Archaeological Unit assisted by the Cambridge University Archaeological Department. Their 'dig' off West Fen Road in 2001, between what is now Berisford Road and the A10 bypass, has revealed that the site, sufficiently densely occupied to justify calling it a town, was in use from the ninth to the twelfth centuries, and that it gradually moved up the slope represented by the modern West Fen Road towards St Etheldreda's church and monastery, attracted by its wealth and protection, shortly after its rebuilding during St Dunstan's Benedictine Revival.

From Stretham the Isle then extended to the west, south of what is now Grunty Fen, and then another great mere, via Wilburton and Haddenham to Earith, curving around north (taking in Sutton, Mepal, Chatteris etc.) and turning east to end at Witchford. On some maps it looks rather like a shoemaker's last. Medieval descriptions of the Isle claim that it extended north to south, from Littleport (or Abbot's Delf) to 'Cotingelade' (somewhere near Cottenham) and west to east from 'Chirchwere' (near Sutton?) to Stretham.

Within the boundaries of the Isle itself, the Fenland Survey (carried out 1981–88) states that some of the islands, such as Coveney, were themselves connected by the causeways, two of which were identified during the survey itself. One trackway, of small pieces of gravelly flint, runs across fen ground from the peninsula on which Witchford stands to Coveney. Another connects two closely adjacent peninsulas between Witchford and Ely. Coveney is connected to the eastern end of Witcham by one and to Wardy Hill by another. The idea of causeways running through the Fens was obviously a well-known concept in the Middle Ages. Wherever King William built his famous causeway or causeways, he could rely on local knowledge to point out to him which were the best routes, and much of his building would have meant strengthening and widening existing tracks. It might be that what Abbot Thurstan did was to send monks to the king to assist in the choice of the best route. It is worth noting that in Matthew Paris (*Chronica Majora* for 1071) it is claimed that:

> The King coming against the Isle with all his forces, butsecarles, footsoldiers and knights, surrounded it by war. Then, building roads of immense length amidst those swamps and costly bridges also, he rendered those profound and watery depths passable by men and beasts, and then erected a castle from its very foundations at a place called Wisbech.

This summary of the affair, late and exaggerated though it is, suggests that there was more than one road (i.e. causeway) and probably more than one attempt to use bridges. It also reveals the development of a myth about the efforts made by the king to overcome the defenders at Ely. If the works constructed at Ely had been on this scale, then the major chroniclers would surely have said more about it than they do.

But the Isle was a prize worth conquering. Not only because of the wealth of the monastery, although control over that would give control over its vast estates, but because the Isle itself was a rich and fertile area of farmland. The knight 'Deda' paints an idyllic picture, partly to discourage the king from continuing with the attack. He had emphasised already the warlike nature of Hereward and his supporters and he then stressed that defenders would never run out of food. He says that, in effect, the blockade is useless. The interior of the Isle is rich in resources, full of all sorts of crops, superior in the richness of its soils to other parts of England with many lovely fields and pastures, with well-known hunting grounds, an ideal breeding ground for cattle and beasts of burden, famous for its woodlands and vineyards. He enumerates the abundant domesticated and wild animals; stags, fallow deer, goats and hares; otters, weasels, stoats and polecats; many varieties of fish, innumerable eels, wolf-fish, pike, perch, roach, burbot and lampreys, even salmon and the royal fish sturgeon. He rhapsodises over the many varieties of birds which can be caught and eaten and ends by saying that the Isle is seven miles in length and four in breadth. Lastly he stresses that the Isle is strongly defended or enclosed by vast meres and wide marshlands as though by a strong wall. If he ever actually said all this then it would be suggested today that, having been Hereward's captive, and courteously entertained (and no doubt led to reveal the strength and dispositions of the king's forces) he was suffering from what is now called the 'Stockholm Syndrome', where the captive comes to side with his captors. His was an exaggerated picture of the Isle, but nevertheless with a great deal of truth in it.

The Fens

The sources also emphasise the dangers of the marshes. They tell how the Normans came to grieve over the deaths of their comrades-in-arms 'sucked down to the bottom of the swirling waters of the mere'. Likewise they say that a man in full armour would find the ground so marshy and unstable that it would scarcely support his weight and was liable to collapse

> like chaos into a whirlpool of solid matter ... disguised all the time by the hazardous beds of flag-iris which customarily provide a cover for the marshy soil.

The beds of these waters are treacherous with 'headlong descents to the abyss ... [which] ... when touched by the slightest fine weather splits open in wide, deep cracks'. The weather, prone to bursts of heavy rain mixed with hail, adds to the hazards and renders the knights exhausted over and over again. They are worn out by 'the narrowings and windings of the causeway' which 'hinder both sight and speech'. This caused the much-disliked Bretons to seek to desert King William until compelled to return to their duty by the king, who refused them access to their boats in which they had hoped to return to Brittany.

Nor was the terror induced by Hereward's customary resort to the tactic of setting fire to the reeds and sedge ignored. The fear of this drove the Normans to their deaths in the swamp, as the firing of the Conqueror's siege towers spread fire into the reed-swamp to an extent of nearly two furlongs. The fire was 'a monstrosity of horrible appearance' which absolutely terrified the soldiers, as did the noise caused by the burning branches of willow which drove them mad. Astbury, in his study *The Black Fen*, confirms how lethal a fen fire in the peat could be. Once fire takes hold it spreads through the peat for hundreds of feet. These fires are long-lived and well-nigh impossible to extinguish. Men attempting to walk across affected areas can fall waist-deep into burning peat. This burns below a crust of waterlogged peat and the application of more water can cause an explosion. Such was the nature of the marshes around the Isle.

The course taken by the River Great Ouse differed completely from the modern route. At that time it entered the Isle at Earith but immediately turned due north, to Benwick, impelled perhaps by its confluence with the Old West River or Westee, which flowed from the watershed, probably at or near the present-day Twenty Pence Bridge near Stretham, due west and then running some four furlongs south of Aldreth. From Earith it meandered its way towards Upwell and Outwell and the Wellstream and from there reached Wisbech. The Cam, then called Granta, flowed north via Upware, reinforced on the other side of the watershed by the Old East River or Estee, passing either around or through the extinct mere of Haveringe to Little Thetford, where nearby there was a chalk and gravel ford and a fishery later called 'Hereward's Reach', and the Wicken Promontory near Fordy (a long finger of higher ground). Then, as it approached Ely it meandered east towards Stuntney, having left Ely near the bridge on the present-day Newmarket Road, continuing north through Rolls or Rollers Lode and Burnt Fen (the course is today visible as a roddon or rodham, a ridge of gravel left by the dried-up course of the river and a tiny stream) to Prickwillow, named variously as Ely Ouse or Prickwillow Ouse, and joined at Prickwillow Bridge by the River Lark, from thence via Littleport to the sea. There was no actual connection between the Great Ouse and the Ely Ouse, and Ely could still only be reached by boat. Only in the twelfth century was a diversion made to bring boats nearer to Ely for the benefit of monks,

townsmen and castlemen. Lower down, the Ten Mile
River was made, a straight length of the Ouse from
Downham Market to King's Lynn.

One or two other places need to be mentioned. Some of
Hereward's raiding took place in the vicinity of 'Reche',
that is Reach, where the king had set up a guard post or
garrison on his way from Cambridge Castle to the Ouse.
He had fortified a section of the Devil's Dyke earthwork
and ditch near Reach Lode, not far from Burwell (which
was itself put to the torch by Hereward), and there was
a skirmish there between a few of Hereward's men and
some two dozen Normans. King William is also said
to have brought materials for his assault works and
causeway construction from 'Cotingelade', (watercourse
of Cotta's people), not the present Cottenham Lode,
which was constructed much later, but some other
waterway. Some have suggested the Car Dyke, which
might then have been useable, or the Beach Ditch (known
as Cottenham Lode in the seventeenth century) which
ran from Cottenham to Stretham. Dugdale's *History of
Embanking* claimed that the Car Dyke ran from 'Beche'
(Landbeach) to Chaff Fen in Cottenham and 'so to
the Ouse' and was then diverted to Harringmere. The
Fenland Survey suggests that Cottenham Lode ran from
Chare Lode in Cottenham and was linked to the West
Water. But the *Liber Eliensis* refers to Cotingelade as a
lake. The question is now almost insoluble, though it
can be suggested that 'Cotingelade' was in some way a
tributary of the Cam.

There are a few other topographical details which have
a bearing on the conflict between Hereward and William
but these are reserved for future discussion of the exact
nature and location of the king's attacks and Hereward's
defence of Ely.

6

Hereward Returns to England

Hereward made a visit to England in between his main engagements in Flanders. On this first visit he is said to have found that his father's lands had been confiscated by the Normans, the foreigners who now ruled England. His younger brother (unnamed) was said to have died at Norman hands and Hereward is alleged to have driven out the Norman occupants, slaying several.

This is presented as an attack on the manor of Bourne which is said to have been his father's residence, but, as has been established, it was Earl Morcar, and not some otherwise unknown 'Leofric of Bourne', who had held it. Morcar's successor was Ogier the Breton. There is no evidence of any attack on Bourne other than the claims of the *Gesta* and 'Ingulf', which on this point are effectively only one source. That Hereward might well have gone to the main residence of his real father, that is Ware in Hertfordshire, is possible but cannot be established. The fourteenth-century annals simply say that Hereward returned from overseas 'to his inheritance', that is his patrimony, and discovering that the Norman King had taken it from him, slew the occupants and moved quickly against the king. If this occurred in 1067 or 1068, it is possible, but not stated anywhere, that he joined the 'Silvatici' and took part in the abortive rising of that year.

Certainly the conditions in England during the first
four years of Norman rule lent themselves to such a
course of action. There was widespread looting and
confiscation, beginning during William's absence in
Normandy for most of 1067, when Odo of Bayeux and
William fitzOsbern, left to govern the realm in the new
king's absence, did little to restrain either the barons
or their soldiery. To which behaviour there was at first
little resistance. No doubt the southern shires were still
reeling from the effects of the defeat at Hastings. It has
been rightly observed that defeat in a major battle has
political consequences; it shakes the national will of the
conquered people and so makes them ready to obey the
conqueror, which explains the extent of collaboration
with the new regime. Orderic Vitalis complains only that
the English were 'groaning under the Norman yoke and
suffering oppressions from the proud lords who ignored
the king's orders'. He also says that as a result of this loss
of liberty the English plotted ceaselessly to find some way
of shaking off the yoke that was so intolerable. There
was even a rumour to the effect that all the Normans
were to be massacred by hostile Englishmen supported
by the Danes.

Many of the rebels prepared to defend themselves in
woods, marshes and creeks, which were seething with
discontent. It is known too that men from the East
Midlands and East Anglia took part in the revolts. So
1068 is the year when royal castles had to be built at
Lincoln, Huntingdon and Cambridge to subdue the area;
accounts suggest that there was trouble for the Normans
around Ely as a result and that thereafter the Normans
kept a watch on the Isle. William found that although
he had, as he thought, completely rid the kingdom of
all his enemies after the failure of the revolt in 1068,
he was still plagued by continual eruptions of trouble.
Some Normans were so frustrated and worried by the

conditions, the fire, rapine and daily slaughter, that they chose to surrender their estates and return to Normandy. The English, on the other hand, were so angered at the loss of patrimonies and the deaths of kinsmen and fellow countrymen, that they forgot fealty, the oaths they had given and all thought of the safety of hostages and again planned revolt. But it can also be said that the rebellions suited one aspect of William's policy. It is certain that he needed not only the prizes of war which he claimed after the battle of Hastings but also the successful defeat of rebellion in order to reward his Norman followers with the lands of the defeated English.

Hereward's First Return

It was during this first return to England that Hereward made contact with his uncle, Abbot Brand. The romanticised version of this meeting given in the *Gesta* and repeated by Ingulf is intended to satisfy twelfth-century audiences and readers that Hereward was a worthy antagonist whom no Norman could have been ashamed to confront. It would have been unacceptable for such luminaries as William de Warenne, Ivo Taillebois, William Malet or Frederick Oosterzele-Scheldewindeke to be found fighting a man who was not a belted knight, nor indeed could King William be expected to deal with such an inferior person as a mere 'thegn'. Thegns, after the Conquest and certainly by the reign of Henry I, were very low down in the social scale. Hereward had to be given a suitable social and military rank. Accordingly, he is presented as approaching the abbot in order to be made a knight and for knighthood to be conferred by a monk from Ely on some of his most doughty followers. There is no evidence of English abbots conferring knighthood, in the continental sense of that word, on English thegns, even king's thegns, before 1066. As the

Council of Westminster in 1102 went out of its way to forbid them to do so in future, it would seem that they had started this after 1066 in order to extend the Church's control over what was, for England, a new kind of status.

Hereward did visit his uncle, possibly simply because he was his uncle, but also perhaps in order to renew his position as 'a man of the monks'. He might have been renewing the terms on which he served the abbey and its abbot, following the death of Abbot Leofric, and securing his rights to his land. This suggests that the ceremony between Brand and his nephew was a renewal of commendation, in which Hereward took the abbot as his lord and Brand accepted him as his man, with all that that implied. The other men would in turn have been renewing their commendation to the abbey of Ely, whose men they probably were.

Having caused the Norman king as much trouble as he could in a short space of time, Hereward apparently decided to return to Flanders, where he took part in the conflict between 'a certain famous knight' called Baldwin and the Vicomte of Picquigny (see Chapter 3). Perhaps he was obliged to do so under the terms under which he served Robert the Frisian. He then recruited some more of his men and returned again to England accompanied by his wife Turfrida. She is said to have eventually parted from Hereward and become a nun at Crowland for at least four years before dying there. Crowland is not recorded as being a double monastery, though such were known in England, where monks and nuns lived their lives in separate buildings, joining together only for services in the monastery church. The truth might well be that after the return to England she took refuge at Crowland while Hereward renewed his conflict with the Normans.

The Second Return

At this point the exact sequence of events becomes both clearer and more opaque. Hereward's second return was probably in the autumn of 1069, although no source claims any participation by him in the great revolt of that year. He was not, as far as the sources are concerned, one of those who joined Edgar Aetheling and his supporters in the welcome extended to Earl Osbjorn and the three sons of Swein of Denmark, nor in their advance on York and co-operation with the Northumbrian rebels. The sources are silent until his presence in England is confirmed by the *Anglo-Saxon Chronicle*. The *Peterborough Chronicle* (E) for 1070, dealing with the appointment of Abbot Turold of Malmesbury to Peterborough, provides the first reference to Hereward in a major source. The monks of Peterborough had learned that 'because they had heard it said that the king had given the abbacy to a French abbot called Turold' therefore 'their own men, namely Hereward and his band (*genge*), wished to plunder the monastery'. They also knew that Turold was already at Stamford in Lincolnshire. The *Worcester Chronicle* (D) confirms that Peterborough was plundered

> by the same men whom Bishop Aethelric had excommunicated earlier because they had carried off everything he possessed.

There are no other details of this episode but Hereward and his men were by now well-known outlaws and this is probably one of their robberies.

What remains to be established, and which, apart from the matter of the robbery of Bishop Aethelric, is not recorded in the major sources, is what Hereward and his men had done to earn their reputation. One clue lies in the contradictions between the two versions of the

Chronicle, supported by the twelfth-century *Chronicle of Hugh Candidus* (or Albus), a Peterborough monk, which put the attack on Peterborough before the siege of Ely and the lesser sources, the *Estorie des Engles* of Master Geoffrey Gaimar and the *Gesta Herewardi*, which put the attack after the siege. Both of these latter sources have other inconsistencies which suggest that they are wrong and the major sources are right. On the other hand, the first view is that of the Peterborough Tradition and the second that of the Ely Tradition. Perhaps, therefore, some of the activities of Hereward should actually be placed before the attack on Peterborough or between that and the events of the siege. A closer inspection of the sources suggests that this was indeed so.

In writing of the actions of Abbot Turold, the *Annales Burgo-Spaldenses* have an entry for 1070 which records that the abbot disposed of sixty-two hides of the abbey's lands to his stipendiary knights as payment for guarding him against Hereward and another, as part of his Obit in 1098, confirms that he enfeoffed his knights and built a castle next door to the abbey (the mound is still there in the Prior's Garden adjacent to the church) which was known as 'Mount Turold'. He obviously found such defensive measures essential. As these actions followed his arrival at Peterborough, and therefore came after Hereward's attack, they occurred either between the attack and the retreat to the Isle of Ely or even during the period when local commanders, who may have included Turold himself, kept a watch on the Isle before King William himself found it necessary to take a hand. The account of events at Peterborough in the chronicle of Hugh Candidus supports the account in the *Annales*.

The story of Hereward's conflict with the Norman regime given in the *Gesta Herewardi* and the *Liber Eliensis*, as well as Geoffrey Gaimar, provides clues about his activities both before and after the attack on

Peterborough. Even William of Malmesbury (in his *Gesta Pontificum*) notes that when Turold was transferred to Peterborough he found the area 'infested with brigands led by a certain Hereward, who was hiding among the marshes'.

One quite major event does appear to fit well into this period of what, to the Normans, was certainly 'brigandage' and that is the assassination of William de Warenne's brother-in-law, Frederick Oosterzele-Scheldewindeke, as a result of which Earl William gained possession of his brother-in-law's lands in England. There is no recorded motive for Hereward's action (or that of a group of his men in an alternative version of the story) but Frederick was in Flanders at the same time as Hereward and the roots of their hostility must lie there. The Warennes also had interests in Flanders; William's wife Gundreda brought him estates near St Omer from the property of Frederick's family.

The *Gesta* puts the killing during Hereward's first return to England, erroneously dated 1069 but actually in 1067. Possibly Frederick had come to England with his brother Gerbod, who was made Earl of Chester. The *Gesta* claims that Frederick was planning to ambush Hereward and, according to that source, take his head to King William, but that the outlaw learned of his intention and, being in Norfolk, turned the tables on him, laying an ambush himself. One version of the tale has Hereward challenge Frederick to a duel which, as Hereward was not a knight, he might well have refused. An ambush is more likely, and the *Gesta* says of Hereward that 'he fell on him and killed him', which explains the *Hyde Chronicle*'s view that Hereward's men were involved. It is known that the ambush and slaying of individual Normans, picking them off one by one, had become a common English pastime which led to the institution of the Murdrum Fine. So many

Normans were turning up dead in places where there were no relatives to avenge the dead man that something had to be done.

After this assassination Hereward returned for the last time to St Omer. Matthew Paris says, probably of this period, that Hereward 'committed many evil deeds to the injury of the king in various places' before ending up at Ely.

It was about this time that Hereward was said to have burned three villages near Bourne before taking up quarters at Ely and that this followed an attempt at an ambush by William de Warenne which happened at a place called 'Herbeche' (which could just mean Holbeach) when Hereward was moving from Bardney to Ely. The burning of the villages, all located near Hereward's former estate at Witham-on-the-Hill, had been set as a signal summoning Hereward's men now that their leader had returned. Hereward and de Warenne apparently confronted each other across a river, leading Warenne to suspect a trap. After an exchange of javelins and insults, Hereward challenged the Norman to cross the river, an offer he, perhaps wisely, declined, so Hereward and his men broke off the engagement and continued on their way to Ely. There they were welcomed by the monks who had heard rumours that Abbot Thurstan was to be replaced by a Norman.

The *Liber Eliensis* claims that the abbot and his monks had actually summoned Hereward and his men (some of whom were probably holding land from the monastery) 'to defend their country and the liberty of their fathers'. They also welcomed the arrival of the Danes, who had come down from the Humber to the Wash in preparation for a return to Denmark in the spring of the next year, offering the Isle as a base.

Hereward and the Danes

No doubt monks from Ely and Hereward and his men were among those who welcomed the arrival of the Danish Fleet when 'the English folk from all the Fenlands came to meet them, thinking that they were sure to conquer the whole land' (*Peterborough Chronicle*, 1070). It could be that the 'folk' here meant not merely people but an armed force because 'folk' is used in the chronicle to mean 'army' just about as often as it means 'people'. Referring to the time just before the Danes arrived, the *Liber Eliensis* says that the Isle was already under siege from about 1069 ('the third year of King William'). As William was heavily engaged elsewhere in that year, any blockade of the Isle would have been undertaken by his local representatives, men like William de Warenne and Ivo Taillebois, or even Harduin de Scales or Richard fitzGilbert (both of whom had land in Cambridgeshire). Hereward is reported by the *Liber Eliensis* as having gone out to meet the enemy with a few of his men, and it is said that he overwhelmed those Normans he encountered and 'destroyed them' while the rest fled. He then returned to Ely with much plunder and:

> His name became known to all and people told the story
> of his battles throughout the Kingdom.

It was during this period that Hereward, acting in conjunction with the Danes, made his attack on Peterborough Abbey. The Peterborough chronicler, who had good reason to know the truth, assigns the attack to the year 1070 (which means that the Ely tradition is clearly wrong). The writer introduces Hereward as leader of a '*genge*', rendered by different translations as gang or band or company, who joins the Danes in an assault on the monastery. The chronicle gives details of the attack, which are confirmed by the *History of the Abbey* written in the twelfth century by the monk Hugh Candidus, the White. The attack occurred shortly before 2 June (by which time, the chronicle says, Abbot Turold had arrived at Peterborough) and so was made at the end of May. After the attack the Danes did not, as no doubt Hereward had intended, stay to launch an attack on the Normans, but returned to Denmark, doubtless on the orders of King Swein who had struck a bargain with the Conqueror, and left Hereward and his companions in the lurch. They also took with them the plunder from the abbey.

The motives of Hereward in carrying out this attack can be pieced together from the events of 1070 and the claims of Hugh Candidus. There seem to have been three reasons for his decision. Firstly, the various sources insist that it was in this year that King William decided to have 'all the monasteries that were in England plundered'. A later writer, Gervase of Canterbury, claims that the king seized the charters and moveable property of the monasteries (which might explain why so many charters had to be replaced, even by wholesale forgery) and 'Florence' of Worcester explains the king's motives. He says that he wanted all the money which the wealthiest English had placed in the monasteries for safe keeping. In the absence of banks, monasteries were used as good places to deposit wealth, trusting in the sanctity of the abbey or priory to deter thieves.

William's action was sheer theft. Much of what would have been taken was not the property of the monks but of those who had left it there, although the Normans were none too scrupulous in distinguishing what was monastic and what was lay property. William no doubt justified his action as the seizure of the wealth of those who had died opposing him, whether in lawful battle or in rebellion. This had the effect of pauperising the heirs of the dead, leaving them destitute and desperate. No doubt the property of those who had fled into exile was also seized. One might see it as an early form of punitive death duties and it completed the expropriation of the defeated English, or at least those who had not collaborated. This goes some way to explain the desperation of those who continued to resist the Conqueror. One effect might have been to cause Edwin and Morcar, who seem to have been in humane if humiliating house arrest at William's court and beginning to fear that they were soon to be imprisoned, to flee the court, probably early in 1071, and seek to join the last rebels.

Some of their wealth had probably been seized in this way, or they had decided to withdraw it from its hiding place so that they could take it with them into exile. Robbery would then become a motive for the slaying of Earl Edwin. So, as Orderic Vitalis laments, 'foreigners grew rich with the spoils of England'.

Meanwhile, King Swein of Denmark had taken a hand in events. He arrived on the Humber where

> the people of the countryside met him and came to terms
> with him thinking that he was sure to conquer the whole
> country.

He was joined by Earl Osbjorn and Bishop Christian of Aarhus and the Danish housecarls and went to Ely where

> Englishmen from all the Fenlands came to meet them
> thinking that they were sure to conquer the whole land.

This meeting involved a considerable body of men, including, it would seem, Hereward and his men. The *Peterborough Chronicle* records that there was a rumour to the effect that 'their own men, namely Hereward and his

companions' wished to plunder the monastery, ostensibly
to prevent the portable wealth of the abbey falling into
the hands of the new Norman abbot, Turold.

This is the second reason for Hereward's intervention.
His uncle, Abbot Brand, had recently died (27 November
1069) and King William had taken the opportunity to
install a Norman as abbot. He chose Turold, then abbot
of Malmesbury. He was a bellicose monk from Fécamp
who had upset the peaceful monks of Malmesbury by
behaving more like a soldier than a monk. William
is reported to have remarked that since Turold liked
fighting he might as well be given someone to fight,
namely Hereward, and appointed him to Peterborough.
William of Malmesbury records that the abbey was in
turmoil at the time as the area was 'infested with brigands
led by a certain Hereward who was hidden among the
marshes'. Hereward would certainly have objected to the
appointment of a Norman to a monastery he regarded
as his own. He was, as Hugh Candidus insists, 'a man
of the monks' and held such of his land as was not from
Crowland from the abbey. It might even be suggested that
he was now in some sense, but not necessarily formally,
a 'protector' or advocate of Peterborough as his father,
Brand's brother Asketil, might in fact have been, judging
from the extent of the lands he held which were returned
to Peterborough by Abbot Brand.

Hugh Candidus reveals the third reason for Hereward's
action; he says that Hereward insisted that his main
motive was to remove the abbey's treasure so that it
would not fall into Norman hands and was doing so out
of loyalty to the abbey, but he also states that Hereward
used the prospect of much plunder to persuade the Danes
to attack Peterborough as well. Hugh Candidus actually
says that while some supported Hereward out of loyalty
to the church, others believed that they would defeat
King William and take possession of the land. It might

be that he hoped to use the riches of Peterborough to bribe the Danes into becoming involved in a war with the Normans. If so, he was to be disappointed.

Even though Turold had not yet arrived, he was said to be near Stamford in Lincolnshire with a force of 160 knights (enough to qualify as a small army by the standards of the time) provided in part by the king, so Hereward and the Danes decided to strike first. They launched an attack in a flotilla of small fen boats, coming along the Wellstream from its junction with the Ouse, and attempted to enter the abbey from the hythes along the river. Repelled at first by the monks, the attackers set fire to the street of houses alongside the abbey, to create confusion, and set fire to the Bolhithe gate which provided access to the abbey enclosure. Once inside they set about collecting everything they could lay their hands on. Hugh Candidus describes the treasure: they tried, and failed, to take the Great Crucifix which hung at the entry to the high altar and so removed the crown from the head of the figure of Christ, with its precious gems, and the 'Scabellus' or foot support at its feet of pure gold inlaid with gems. They seized two 'feretories' (boxes used to transport the relics of saints) of gold and nine others of silver and gold also encrusted with jewels, twelve jewelled crosses and other golden objects and others of gold and silver, all decorated with precious stones, together with ornaments of all kinds and even books (which often had jewelled covers). Finally they went up into the tower of the church and removed the great decorated altar frontal which had been hidden there by the monks. Also among all this plunder were items the monks would have regarded as even more precious: the relics of saints, such as the arm of St Oswald, preserved by the monks and used to attract pilgrims to visit the church.

Leaving the area around the monastery devastated by fire and the church stripped of its riches, the raiders retreated, taking with them Adelwold (Aethelwold) the Prior and many senior monks, perhaps as hostages. The rest of the community were dispersed, all save one man, Leofwine the Tall, who was left behind because he lay sick in the infirmary. Despite the robbery and the burning of the houses of the abbey's dependants, no other serious damage was done. The fabric of the monastery itself and its church was unharmed so that Turold when he arrived was able to resume normal monastic services within a week. It was Turold himself who destroyed the existing monastery and built a new one complete with the great abbey church in the new Norman style.

Then, from Hereward's point of view, it all went wrong. He and the Danes retreated to Ely with their booty and their clerical hostages. The Danes took possession of all the treasure and stored it on their ships, so that Hereward could not easily get at it. King William made overtures to King Swein, who came to an agreement with him that, in return for being permitted to retain the plunder of gold and silver they had already accumulated, the Danes would return to Denmark. Paying a short visit to the Thames before departure, the Danes duly left, taking the plunder of Peterborough (and no doubt from other places also) and Aethelwold and a few monks with them. The rest were released at Hereward's insistence to return to Peterborough. It is doubtful whether Swein ever intended an invasion as opposed to the usual Danish practice of deep, penetrating raids to grab as much as they could.

Swein's venture turned out less profitable than he had hoped. While they were at sea returning to Denmark a great storm arose and scattered the Danish fleet, some ending up in Norway or even Ireland, and a few limping back to Denmark. Little of the treasure survived except a 'great table' (probably the altar frontal is meant) and some of the crucifixes and feretories. Aethelwold and his companions survived and managed to hang on to some

of the relics, especially the Arm of St Oswald. Even in
Denmark more loss was sustained. The Danes got drunk
and carelessly set fire to the church on one of Swein's
royal manors where the plunder was stored so that the
church and all it contained was destroyed. Aethelwold
and his monks were allowed to return home, again
following some sort of agreement between Hereward
and the Danes, and took the relics with them. They took
refuge at first at Ramsey, where they left the relics in the
keeping of the abbot. Perhaps they preferred Ramsey to
Peterborough under Turold. The relics were later restored
to Peterborough, but only after Turold had threatened
to burn down Ramsey. In the traditions of Peterborough
and Malmesbury, Hereward's activities are condemned
as those of a petty thief (*latrunculus*) and his men are
malefactors, quite different from the view of him by the
monks of Ely as their heroic defender.

That Hereward's attack had not been an act of random
vandalism is suggested by the fact that the monastery,
although robbed, was not destroyed, that none of the
monks seem to have been harmed and that Hereward
was able to secure the return home of Prior Aethelwold
and his companions. The actions were aimed purely at
the Normans.

Possibly as a result of all this, King William imposed
military service on all the monasteries of south England
around this time, requiring them to provide quotas of
knights for his service. Peterborough and (for a time) Ely
were required to provide sixty knights when the highest
demand elsewhere was for forty. This was partly because
of the importance of these monasteries as part of the
eastern defences and partly, in Ely's case, as a punitive
quota imposed as a result of rebellion.

Hereward and his men, and no doubt other Peterborough
tenants who might also have been involved, now had no
option but to hold out at Ely and await King William's

reaction. It was not long in coming. He apparently ordered some 'brave and strong men ... to gather together from towns and villages' to attack Hereward and his men and take their position by storm. This would mean the local commanders in the shires around the Fens. Hereward's own men, having spied on their attackers, despaired of being able to resist, but he was enraged. He is said to have fallen on them and struck them down, dispatching some to death in the water, and so delivered his men from fear, making a great speech to encourage them, full of biblical allusions. This was the usual conventional battle address put into a commander's mouth by classical authors from whom medieval writers borrowed style and material.

The *Liber Eliensis* has the king's advisors suggest that peace be offered to these rebels because the Isle was too well fortified and these men were only defending the 'heritage of their fathers', implying that continued efforts to deal with Hereward at that time were considered too costly to be worthwhile. The king is said to have agreed, and agents were sent offering a truce which Hereward accepted, agreeing to cease pillaging, presumably on condition that he and his men were left alone. This story might be an attempt to explain William's delay in tackling Hereward. It might also be the basis of the claims made by other writers that Hereward was reconciled to King William. Hereward was certainly never reconciled to the king before the affair at Ely, as his attack on Peterborough shows. He is equally unlikely to have been reconciled to him afterwards. None of the other laymen involved were permitted to submit and be reconciled: the leaders, Morcar, Bishop Aethelwine and Siward Barn were all imprisoned. Earl Edwin, who had fled earlier, was assassinated, and though the 'common people' were released unharmed, all those who had positions of responsibility and had taken a leading part in opposing the king, no doubt including those of Hereward's leading supporters who had failed to escape with him, lost not only their lands but hands, feet and eyes. It is not very likely that Hereward would have been treated any better, William had lost too many young men in his campaign at Ely.

The people of the Isle continued to distrust the Normans because of their known ferocity and intolerable despotism and continued to keep a sharp lookout on all approaches to the Isle. The *Liber Eliensis* connects this to the later events at Ely by insisting that the 'nobles', meaning possibly Morcar and his associates, broke this truce, even gouging out the eyes or cutting off the hands and feet of captured Normans. This may have been inserted in order to offer some justification for the way William treated his captives after Ely had fallen. An element of confusion arises here as the people of Ely are represented as recalling Hereward to their aid after hearing of the death in captivity of Bishop Aethelwine, but this can be explained as another example of the tendency of the writer of the *Liber Eliensis* to misdate events when he was unsure of their exact sequence. Hereward's 'recall' would then mean his decision to join forces with Morcar after the meeting at Welle.

7

Hereward Defies
the Conqueror

Deserted, then, by their untrustworthy allies, the Danes, Hereward and his outlaw band, supported, according to some sources, by numerous members of his own kin and by other tenants of Peterborough, remained at Ely. They had been invited there in the first place, as the *Liber Eliensis* asserts, because the people of Ely placed great trust in Hereward and his militia. From the Isle, Hereward sent out messages to gather together

> from everywhere kinsmen and freemen whom the king had condemned to be exiled and disinherited, and their company was strengthened in opposition to their enemies.

Some of the kinsmen and allies of Hereward can be identified. Perhaps the most formidable, and useful to Hereward, was Thorkell 'of Harringworth', also called Thorkell or Turchil the Dane, from Northamptonshire. He held land at Leighton Bromeswold and was the most powerful king's thegn in the Eastern Danelaw. He had gone 'over to the Danes who were his kinsmen' after fleeing from many of his lands after the Conquest. He was probably the son of Cnut's man, Thorkell the Tall, who ruled East Anglia. After the fall of Ely his lands went to Earl Waltheof, as did those of others who had been at Ely. He had owned lands of 'baronial' extent, some 134 hides and 138 carucates in eight shires.

Another prominent supporter was the thegn Siward of Maldon, who had wide estates in East Anglia and was known as '*socius Herewardi*', that is comrade or companion. He held some ninety hides and twenty-five carucates in several shires. Then there were two relatives of Morcar. Firstly Godric of Corby, who is called his '*nepos*', that all-purpose word which here seems to mean cousin. He was probably a son of Earl Aelfgar's eldest son, Burgheard, who died in 1061. The second is Tosti or Tostig 'of Davenesse' (usually identified as Daventry). He is called 'cognatus' of Earl Tostig Godwinson and said to have been named for him at baptism.

Another leading supporter is called Ordgar. This is probably King Edward's Sheriff of that name, who had been Harold's man also. Early in William's reign he still controlled the eight-and-a-half hundreds of the 'Soke' or Liberty of Bury St Edmunds. He forfeited his lands and office, as Sheriff of Cambridgeshire, after the fall of Ely. Then there is 'Turbertinus' (Thorbeorht?) from Freckenham in Suffolk. A writ (No. 47) *c.* 1071 for Archbishop Lanfranc says that the Archbishop is to have Freckenham 'as Harold held it and Turbartus and Gotinus of Harold'. Presumably the latter two are sons of Orthi who held Freckenham before 1066. Land in Isleham, Cambridgeshire, was taken from Wulfric, King Edward's huntsman, who held it under his 'Thurbert'.

Then there are the relatives of Hereward himself. The Flanders narrative in the *Gesta* names two paternal cousins, Siward Rufus (the Red) and Siward Blond (the White), who shared his adventures there and returned with him to England. In the list of Hereward's 'men' come the twins Outi (or Auti) and Duti, his nephews, and Winter and Liveret, who are described as kinsmen.

There are about thirty individuals listed in the *Gesta*
and several in Gaimar, of whom nothing is known. They
seem to be put in to fill out the account of his supporters
(see Appendix). A few are identified in a manner which
suggests that they might be real figures, such as Rahere,
the Heron, from 'Wrokeshambridge', that is Wroxham
on the Bure in the Broads, Brother Siward of Bury
St Edmunds, and Rahenaldus (Reginald), Steward
of Ramsey Abbey. There was a man of this name (as
Reinaldus) who became a monk at Ramsey, eventually
becoming its Dapifer or steward.

For at least the remainder of 1070 and into 1071,
Hereward held out at Ely but, not content merely to
hold the Isle and its monastery so that they would not
fall easily into Norman hands, he also went onto the
offensive. As the *Liber Eliensis* maintains, he carried
out 'pillaging raids and depredations far and wide, a
hundred men at a time, or more than that'. Sometimes
there were heavy losses and the outlaws had to retreat
to the safety of the Isle, but the offensive reassured many
people and some placed themselves under the protection
of the forces on the Isle, even bringing their money and
valuables with them for safe keeping.

One of these could have been Archbishop Stigand,
who is reported to have visited the monastery at about
this time, shortly after his deposition, and left his treasure
there in the keeping of the abbot. The *Liber Eliensis* talks
of his fleeing from place to place and finding nowhere
to hide himself and his possessions, information about
Stigand which is not recorded elsewhere. The Ely story
is that he sent word to Abbot Ecgfrith of St Albans to
bring his, Stigand's, treasures to Ely along with the relics
of St Alban. The abbot is supposed to have done so and
to have left the relics in a small church in the locality.
After Stigand's deposition, and that of the abbot himself,
the relics were then transferred to the safe keeping of

Ely, as the abbot Ecgfrith wished to deprive St Albans of the relics because he had been deprived of his abbacy. However, this part of the story is contradicted by the traditions of St Albans itself. But that Ecgfrith smuggled some of Stigand's property into Ely still remains a real possibility.

Hereward Invokes St Etheldreda

Although recruits appear to have been plentiful, Hereward was not prepared to accept all and sundry into his company. Instead, he imposed a test: only those who were prepared to pledge their loyalty, to Hereward and his immediate allies presumably, by swearing an oath 'upon the body of the most holy virgin Aethelthryth' (Saint Etheldreda) to devote their strength and energy of mind to the defence of the Isle were acceptable. Hereward and his men knew to their cost that some might not otherwise be trustworthy. So the holy virgin became patroness of English opposition to the Normans.

Meanwhile King William was probably quite satisfied that he had subdued all meaningful opposition. The North had been pacified in the Roman manner, 'create a desert and call it peace', and the Danish king and the menace of his fleet had been seen off in the traditional way, by allowing him to leave peacefully with his booty just as Aethelraede had paid off his predecessors with Danegeld. The Norman regime had survived the major test, from within, of its stability. It remained for the new king to face his external enemies. But before he could do so, this last real outburst of English hostility had to be contained.

The Earls Edwin and Morcar, despite repeated submissions, had remained disaffected. After the coronation of William's wife, Matilda, at Whitsun 1068, the earls deserted William's court and returned to their earldoms to lead local resistance which formed round them. This collapsed as soon as William came marching north, building castles as he progressed. The earls renewed their submission. So subdued were the earls that they appear to have taken no part in the subsequent rebellion of 1069–70. However, they had become increasingly unhappy and discontented. Edwin had seen his hopes of a marriage to one of William's daughters, which he had been given to understand was on offer, disappear and had suffered the ravaging of part of his earldom and even the loss of extensive lands with the creation of the marcher earldoms of Chester, Shrewsbury and Hereford. Morcar had seen himself ignored, and much of his earldom granted away to Robert de Commines, which led to the great rising and the devastation of Yorkshire and other northern and midland shires. Even after the rebellion had been put down, it was Waltheof who became Earl of Northumbria, not Morcar.

Edwin and Morcar Desert the King

Either late in 1070 or early in 1071 the earls became aware of rumours that William intended to have them arrested and imprisoned, so they fled again from court, going their different ways through woods and across open country. Orderic Vitalis suggests that they were on the run for some six months, in effect they had gone '*silvaticus*'. The exact sequence of events cannot be untangled with certainty, but during their travels the brother earls joined forces with Bishop Aethelwine, the outlawed bishop of Durham, and a wealthy northern thegn called Siward Barn who had joined the remnants of the northern rebels at Wearmouth, but had decided not to follow Edgar Aetheling and Sheriff Maerleswein to Scotland. This group, with a substantial force of fighting men (the *Peterborough Chronicle* says 'many hundreds'), mainly drawn from the ranks of their own men, took ship and intended to seek exile abroad. The bishop is said to have actually set out for Scotland or Denmark but was turned back by storms. In view of this they had decided to seek shelter on the Isle of Ely, where they could spend the winter before going abroad.

According to Geoffrey Gaimar they all met at a place called 'Welle'. This was most likely somewhere on the 'Wellstream' near Outwell and Upwell in Norfolk. In this version of events Bishop Aethelwine, with his 'companions' (possibly some of the men of St Cuthbert) and Siward Barn had come down from Scotland and encountered Earl Morcar and his thegns. They also joined forces with other Englishmen 'who were outlaws to King William', led by a '*gentilzhom*' who is '*un des meillures del région*' called Hereward, that is a man of gentle or noble birth who was one of the leading men of that district. Other sources describe Hereward as a '*vir strenuissimus*', a most active or energetic man. It is at this point that the *Liber Eliensis* causes some confusion, because it insists on the presence of Earl Edwin, not only at the beginning but even throughout the siege.

All other sources are agreed that Edwin did not stay and even the *Liber*, quoting from Florence of Worcester, states that he parted company from his brother and went north to seek the help of King Malcolm of Scotland. The unknown source from which the *Liber* obtained the idea that Edwin stuck it out with the rest is plainly wrong, but he might have been at Ely rather longer than the other sources suggest. That there were misleading accounts of Edwin's activities is also confirmed by Orderic Vitalis. He has Edwin still active after the siege and making an attempt to rescue Morcar from prison. But he agrees with all the other major sources that Edwin was betrayed by his own men and slain by a band of Norman knights.

What does ring true in Orderic's story is his reference to Edwin spending some six months more or less 'on the run' while seeking help from all over, from the Scots, the Welsh and the Danes (which really belongs to the period just before the siege) and his eventual death, trapped between a rising high tide and a tidal stream which prevented his escape. If his route north, after leaving Morcar possibly at Welle or even after a brief visit to Ely, took him anywhere near the Wash, which came much further inland at that time, then he could certainly have been trapped by the tides.

So the last remnants of English opposition to King William were now all gathered in one place, the formidable and almost impregnable fortress which was the Isle of Ely with its equally defensible fenland monastery. All sources are agreed that the rivers, meres and marshes surrounding the Isle made it a tremendous obstacle, especially to an army whose strength lay in the use of cavalry. The logical mode of attack was by water. But any attempt to get onto the Isle by boat could be repelled. The available ways onto the Isle, from Willingham or Earith, Soham or Downham, were well known and could easily be guarded. The sources are clear that the defenders built bulwarks of peat and wood in the most obviously suitable places, from which javelins and arrows and all sorts of missiles could be fired.

Hereward and his band had, seemingly, already held out for some months against William's local commanders such as Abbot Turold, William de Warenne (of Castle Acre) and Ivo Taillebois. They had caused much 'wearisome trouble' and successfully used 'many insidious stratagems'. Ely would be a hard nut to crack. A siege proper would be a long, drawn-out and wearisome affair because the Isle was well stocked with food.

The King Decides to Act

William had other, more important matters to attend to. His presence was required back in Normandy to ensure his control over the duchy which was under threat from Maine; Malcolm Canmore was a constant threat from Scotland and that area, too, needed to be stabilised, and, although the Danes had returned home, they could just as easily come back. During 1071 the king did, it seems, pay a short visit to Normandy and carried out successful negotiations with Philip of France.

William, on his return, realised that the presence of a large fighting force, led by the remainder of the English leadership, and commanded in the field, as Magister Militum, by a man who had established a reputation as a determined opponent of Norman rule and who had learnt his trade as a warrior in Flanders Fields, would continue to be a magnet for the disinherited and disaffected. Exiles could organise a return and Ely could be reinforced by water by the Danes. There were said to be at least 8,000 men in exile on the continent and they could recruit mercenaries to increase their strength. It is probable that only the comparative rapidity with which William was able to overcome Ely, and the absence of a major figure in exile to organise an invasion, prevented further trouble. As it was, the rest of William's reign was never as quiet as it appeared, and the Danes remained a constant threat.

All sources again agree that the news of the gathering of the king's enemies provoked a major determined response. To describe what then happened in summary form is easy enough, and that is what all the major chroniclers do. The version in the *Peterborough Chronicle* 'E' will suffice:

> But when King William heard of this, he ordered out naval and land levies and surrounded the district, building a causeway as he advanced deeper into the Fens, while the naval force remained to seaward. Then all the outlaws surrendered to him, namely Bishop Aethelwine and Earl Morcar and all their followers except Hereward alone and

all who wished to follow him; and he courageously led
their escape.

Florence of Worcester adds the detail that the causeway
was two miles long, which might be an exaggeration, and
that the attack was from the west, which seems to be an
error.

What no major source does is state exactly where this
famous causeway was. That there was a 'causeway' is
confirmed by a writ issued by King William addressed to
Archbishop Lanfranc, the Count of Mortain and Bishop
Geoffrey of Coutances in 1082 (*Regesta* No. 155). At the
end it says, 'Lastly, those men are to maintain the causeway
at Ely who, by the King's command, have done so hitherto.'
But whether the causeway mentioned in the writ was built
before or after the fall of Ely is uncertain. Probably, King
William constructed several such ways of a temporary
nature and ordered a more permanent way on to the Isle
to be constructed after the fighting was over. To discover
more it is necessary to turn to the pages of the *Liber Eliensis*
and the *Gesta Herewardi*.

Those two documents, the former from a twelfth-
and the latter from a thirteenth-century manuscript, are
essentially one source because their accounts of events at
Ely are derived from an earlier work which has long since
disappeared but which may be, with some reservations,
identified as the 'little work' of Brother Richard of Ely
(not the abbot of that name) containing 'the deeds of
Hereward himself' and written some time before the
Liber Eliensis was compiled. 'Compiled' rather than
written, since the scribe says explicitly that he has taken
his facts from a number of histories, '*e pluribus historiis*',
and has done so 'in summary fashion' using 'brief and
tiny extracts' from 'numerous large-scale sources' (some
of which have been identified) and so avoiding 'things
that are beyond belief'.

The result of this method of working, in the absence of any real historical instinct such as was possessed by William of Malmesbury, for instance, and equally in the absence of any chronological framework, was that the compiler, when writing Book Two of the *Liber*, which contains the matter of the siege, simply took the deeds of Hereward, attributed to 'Leofric the Deacon', as far as they concerned the siege of Ely, and, while altering the style to harmonise with the rest of his writing, inserted into it what he considered were interesting or important pieces of information from other sources. These additions are often clearly distinguishable, especially as they are frequently out of their proper chronological context, as when he writes about the making of Domesday Book which did not occur until 1085. He also wrote a text of the *Gesta Herewardi* based on that of Leofric the Deacon, to which he added material from the anecdotes related to him by the older monks at Ely and a number of surviving members of Hereward's company. This work lies behind the text of the *Gesta* as we have it in Richard of Swaffham's Register.

In addition to the matter from the original *Gesta Herewardi*, the compiler also had access to two other accounts of the siege. One was of Norman origin and describes events from that point of view, possibly deriving from a version put about by some of the knights of the garrison left behind by the king. The other, perhaps derived from some local text, not now extant, contains an account of a laborious crossing of the marsh to Witchford and the betrayal of the defenders by Abbot Thurstan, who tells the king the best way to get his men onto the Isle in return for the restoration of the abbey's lands.

These three versions, plus quotations from Florence, Orderic Vitalis and William of Poitiers (used out of context in order to borrow the language used) and from various biblical texts, especially the Books of Maccabees, are simply written up as though they make one continuous narrative. This has the effect of presenting the reader with successive and differing accounts of the same events and makes the whole affair appear to have taken much longer than it would have done in fact. Any attempt to provide a coherent account of the siege must acknowledge these facts. Because the material is presented in this way it is possible to collate it with that contained in the *Gesta Herewardi*, eliminate the impression of unnecessary repetitions found in both texts and produce an account which makes military, topographical and historical sense.

King William's First Moves

Sometime in the autumn of 1071, King William gathered together an army supported by a fleet and prepared to blockade the Isle of Ely. 'Blockade' is perhaps a more suitable word than 'siege' since the king could not in fact have surrounded the whole Isle as one would surround a castle or a town. In fact the sources say that he set guards on all the (known) exits, or as Geoffrey Gaimar puts it, 'all the passages through the woods were guarded and the marshes round about were vigilantly watched'. There is a clue as to the shires involved in providing the king with men. The *Gesta Herewardi*, in telling its tale of Hereward's adventures in the Brunneswald, relates that when Hereward escaped from Ely, King William gathered an army from surrounding counties to hunt him down. This is an unlikely response by William to deal with one outlaw and his band, but the list of shires involved may echo the list of those who provided men for the attack on Ely. They came from Northamptonshire, Cambridgeshire, Lincolnshire (including Holland, which was controlled by Ivo Taillebois), Huntingdonshire, Leicestershire and Warwickshire.

It is worth noting that Norfolk and Suffolk were not involved directly, perhaps because William did not trust the

Bretons who controlled large parts of these shires under Earl Ralph, son of Ralph the Staller. The contribution from these shires came in the form of the men of William de Warenne from Castle Acre, Richard fitzGilbert of Clare and William Malet from his castle at Eye.

Certainly the king gathered a large force and had 'mighty men' with him. His first base was the castle at Cambridge from which he set out, as Orderic Vitalis states, by way of '*Gronte fluminis*', the River Granta, now better known as the Cam. From there he moved the army from his 'first camp', probably at Reach near the Devil's Dyke, 'towards the Isle near to the River Ouse'. This cannot mean the Old West River near Aldreth because the defenders are described as watching Norman soldiers 'carrying a heap of wood and sand in sacks' with the aim of 'making the bed of the swirling river fordable'. The Aldreth area is far too flat to suggest a 'swirling river' and, together with the assertion that this was on the Ouse, better fits a site below the confluence of the Cam with the several unnamed tributaries which produced the river flowing past Ely, just in front of the Stuntney peninsula. Nor does this look like an attempt, as yet, to construct a causeway. This rather unorganised attempt to ford the Ouse seems to have got nowhere because the defenders had erected defences made of peat from which they could repel attacks from the river. It became obvious to the Normans that footsoldiers would never be able to gain a foothold against determined opposition and cavalry, of course, could not be used.

The account of the *Liber Eliensis* at this point veers off into an account meant to prove that the attack on Ely began in 1069, in accordance with the writer of this passage's desire to establish a comparison between the 'siege' of Ely and the siege of Troy (which lasted seven years). This source has the affair at Ely run from 1069 to 1075 by adding the Revolt of the Earls to the story of the struggle in the Fens. The compiler of the *Liber* therefore uses material which probably belongs to the period when Hereward was holding out at Ely alone after the Danes had left, possibly to establish Hereward as a formidable and commanding figure, and then returns to his main narrative.

That material is then followed by an extensive use of Florence of Worcester's account of the attack on Ely, together with its notorious claim that William built a causeway two miles long on the western side of the Isle. The *Liber* insists that the defenders built here their own siege works made of blocks of peat from behind which they could resist the Norman attack. Such structures would not have left any evidence of their existence for very long. Weathering would soon wear them away. The idea of a two-mile causeway best fits a new approach, bringing up reserves of men and cavalry from Cambridge by way of Willingham and Belsar's Hill. This latter was an Iron Age round work which would have provided William with a ready-made area he could use as a base by surrounding it with a palisade, so constructing a '*castellum*' (a word which applies to a palisade rather than to a motte and bailey). The causeway would have been made by widening and strengthening the existing winding track from Belsar's Hill to the Old West River somewhere near Aldreth, where the Aldreth High Bridge was built much later. The existing track is described by the *Gesta* as 'comparatively useless and narrow and near to a great (unnamed) river' and therefore in need of both strengthening and widening if cavalry were to use it. Fen causeways were customarily built by laying down masses of alder branches over which were laid reeds and rushes, so providing a buoyant layer which would not sink into the mire.

This interpretation of William's actions is supported by the *Gesta Herewardi*'s account which has the king move his army from Reach, near Burwell, to a place where the fen was only four furlongs wide and there, requiring all the fishermen in the area to provide boats, he brought up all kinds of materials, piles of wood and stones and sticks and trunks of trees or great pieces of timber, lashing them together from underneath with cowhides. The *Gesta* maintains that sheepskins filled with air were used to give buoyancy to parts of the structure, which had to cross marshy ground, but the *Liber* says they were full of sand, which is more probable. Perhaps both were used. This attempt is said to have been made at 'Alrehede', usually taken to be Aldreth; the name means 'landing place of the alders'. There is a problem in accepting Aldreth as the location in that the fen there was more like sixteen than four furlongs wide, an echo of Florence of Worcester's 'two miles'. The place name Aldreth in its several forms is not recorded before the twelfth century, so that the identification of 'Alrehede' remains doubtful. (The earliest record of the name is 'Alrehed' in the Pipe Roll 26 Henry II.) Aldreth is also about seven miles from Ely, yet William is said to have attacked much nearer Ely than anyone expected. The site, wherever it was, was chosen because the location was not entirely surrounded by water and swamp (one of the many patches of marginally higher ground) and the marsh less wide than elsewhere, and estimated at four furlongs which was probably an underestimate. Another difficulty is that the causeway ends at the site of the later Aldreth High Bridge, which is some distance to the east of the present hamlet called Aldreth.

The king is said to have put his army ashore a second time by using a causeway, near Aldreth, across a 'causeway he had made ready some time previously'. This first attempt was a disaster. Possibly this 'causeway-cum-bridge', with the characteristics of both, was constructed too hurriedly or perhaps some of the English fishermen recruited to help build it indulged in some sabotage, because when the Norman knights and men-at-arms rushed onto this 'pathway through the swamps', desiring, it was said, to get at the rich plunder of gold and silver they expected to find hidden on the Isle, they overloaded the structure and it collapsed, jettisoning the leaders and those who followed after into the water where 'they were swallowed up in the waters and deep swamp' and only the knight Deda managed to struggle onto drier, firmer ground, because he was first to cross. There he was taken prisoner by those defending the Isle against any attempt to land there, as this was one of the places, and there must have been several, where defensive works made of peat had been prepared, forming 'bulwarks and ramparts'. Deda was taken to Hereward and the English leaders at Ely. The author of the *Gesta* even claimed that in his own day the bodies of the dead were still being drawn up out of the waters, complete with rotting armour (presumably of leather rather than metal). If this was near Aldreth, or to be more exact Aldreth High Bridge at the end of the route from Willingham, then this first rather jerry-built structure was over-extended because the fen at that point was so wide. That would also help to explain the collapse.

The accounts in the *Liber* and the *Gesta* here are substantially the same, except that the *Liber* asserts that this was the king's second attempt to put an army ashore, across a causeway which he had made ready sometime previously, which suggests that he had been strengthening the route from Willingham to Aldreth at the same time as moving another detachment of his forces from Reach to the Ouse where the first inefficient attempt had been made. That first effort was probably a feint made to probe the strength of the resistance and to distract the defenders from the major effort at 'Alrehede'. Nonetheless, it had been a setback for William, who is said to have retreated to 'Branduna', where he grieved over his losses. As this failed attempt had possibly been made on the Old West River it is more probable that he had gone to the Royal Manor of Brampton near Huntingdon rather than Brandon in Suffolk, both places are 'Brantuna' in Domesday Book.

8

King William Frustrated

While the king was, like Achilles, sulking in his tent, the knight Deda, captured when the first causeway collapsed, was entertained by Hereward and the English at Ely. Hereward treated Deda well; in fact, in accord with the 'knightly code' of conduct he would have encountered in Flanders. Then, having shown him the resources of the Isle, and demonstrated the strength of the garrison, he even allowed him to dine in the monastery refectory with the abbot and his monks, Morcar and the other leaders with their men. Then Deda was released and sent back to William. Deda had taken careful note of all he was shown and Hereward would have made sure he saw what he was intended to see.

It was Deda's description of the scene in the refectory, suitably described in terms understood by a twelfth-century audience, that was to form the basis for the 'Tabula Eliensis'. Deda pictures the monks and 'knights' dining together in pairs with shields and lances behind them on the walls and other armour readily accessible nearby. He says that he met the Earls Morcar and Edwin, another called Tosti (presumably the 'Tostii/Tostig of Davenesse' mentioned earlier) and the 'proceres' or noblemen Ordgar and Thurkill. The Tabula is a painting showing alternating pairs of monks and knights, each

of whom is named, and in its present form is a work
of the early Tudor Period, probably Henry VII, though
possibly based on an earlier version, approximately from
the fourteenth century. It seems certain to have been
made by someone who had read the story of Deda in
the *Gesta Herewardi*. This part of the *Gesta* was not
used by the compiler of the *Liber Eliensis*, who in his
text tries to play down the part played by the monks in
the resistance.

On his return, Deda was taken before King William,
who was holding a Council of War in which such
prominent men as William de Warenne and Ivo Taillebois
were discussing the problems posed to Norman rule by
the resistance of Ely. He is welcomed back as one who
has returned from the dead because everyone thought
he was one of those 'sucked down to the bottom of the
swirling water of the mere' (not, be it said, the river).

William complains that he cannot leave this pocket of
resistance at Ely, although he has other urgent matters
to attend to. He says he needs to move against the
Danish army and then go to Normandy and is minded
to offer them peace terms. This may represent another
chronological error by the writer of the *Gesta* or, if his
source mentioned 'Northmen', refer to William's desire
to settle matters with Malcolm of Scotland. The reference
to Normandy also looks forward to the need to set things
in order there before dealing with the problem of Maine.
His councillors, in the *Liber*, stress that to leave these
men undefeated would be to suffer a blow to the Norman
prestige and encourage men to mock the king. Others,
described as 'plunderers of other men's possessions' and
who 'fear losing them if peace is made', support these
arguments. They also complain that the men of the Isle
had been invading many of their estates and the king is
persuaded to make another attack although he is still,
despite his anger, convinced that he cannot take the Isle

because it is so well fortified 'by the power of God' (and St Aethelthryth).

Ivo Taillebois is insistent that a new attempt be made and recommends the services of 'an old woman' (elsewhere called a witch or pythoness) who will cast spells and curse the defenders, so crushing all their courage and weakening their will to resist. He was to some extent opposed by 'Richard, son of Viscount Osbert' (who cannot otherwise be identified), the survivor of the skirmish which, he now reported, had taken place at Reach. He reported that the nearby village of Burwell had been burnt to the ground by Hereward and his men. He related that he and others guarding the palisade erected on Devil's Dyke watched as seven mighty warriors approached in a boat and came against them and that he and nine others endeavoured to engage them, but all except Richard were killed. He only escaped because Hereward intervened, as it was unfair for seven to fight one man, and let him go, presumably so that he could tell what happened. Hereward and his men were then attacked by a larger Norman force from the base camp and retreated to their boats, disappearing into the Fens.

The Second Causeway

Despite this, the king agreed to a renewed assault, gathering reinforcements, renewing the blockade on the Isle and again approaching 'Alrehede'. Here there is a problem of topography. Although a reference is made once more to the commandeering of fishermen and their boats to bring materials from 'Cotingelade', a clear reference to a Lode or waterway near Cottenham (Cotingelade means 'watercourse of Cotta's people' as Cottenham is 'settlement of Cotta's people'), the *Gesta* text here is read by several transcribers as '*Alreheche*' which would mean 'Alor-Reach' or 'stretch of river where the Alders grow',

which is by no means specific. A close inspection of the
text of the *Gesta* shows that the name is 'Alrehethe'.
(The misreadings arise from the use of uncial script. The
uncial letter 'e' has faded and can be confused with 'c'.)
The subsequent text points to a renewed attempt to cross
near Aldreth on the Old West River. The major problem
was how to cross the river itself, which required some
kind of bridge at the end of the causeway.

While the new structure, a much more elaborate
one, is being built, Hereward is described as himself
acting as a spy, in disguise first as a potter then as a
fisherman. Although he might have done this, it should
be remembered that this kind of story is told of many
heroic leaders, notably Alfred the Great, and may be
an 'entertainment' put in to amuse the twelfth-century
readership. In this disguise he is said to penetrate the
Norman camp at 'Branduna', where he learns of the plan
to use the witch against the defenders. He spies on her
preparations. She goes to some nearby springs and begins
casting spells in which she questions 'the Watchman in
charge of the springs' (that is the Guardian Spirit) which
threatens to kill her but is placated by her replies. (There
are recorded instances in pagan times of belief in the
power of 'Guardians' who watch over springs of water.
The monk writing this account would have played down
the real significance of this incident which he would not
have readily invented.)

Next day Hereward had various adventures. One man
seeing him remarks on his resemblance to 'the mighty
Hero, Hereward', but others refuse to believe he could
be this 'ugly rustic' and he pretends not to understand
French, instead claiming, in English, a desire for revenge
on 'that man of Belial' because he had robbed him. Later,
others of the crowd, from the royal kitchens, pick on him
as a stupid idiot, they seize his pots, push him around
and blindfold him so that he breaks his own pots, then

punch and pummel him, pulling hairs out of his beard and trying to shave the crown of his head (give him a tonsure), in fact treating him like a lay Christ-figure. At the end he fights back, pulling off the blindfold and laying about him with a stake from the fireplace. They attack with two- and three-pronged forks but he kills one and wounds several until the guards arrive and arrest him. When one guard threatens to chain him up, Hereward snatches his sword, kills the man with his own weapon, wounds others and escapes. Finding his horse Swallow where he had left her, he escapes into the woods at Somersham (confirming the idea that this happened at Brampton) and returns to Ely, where he gives orders for armed men to keep a close look-out all around the Isle. King William is said to have been impressed by Hereward's exploits.

Although the story has been heavily embroidered to the greater glory of Hereward, and of King William who ultimately defeated him, there may be a kernel of truth in the idea of Hereward having spied on the Norman camp or sent out men to do so and learned of their plans to use a witch, since Hereward is said to have known where the attack was to occur and to have taken measures to thwart it.

More importantly, the king's orders were being carried out. He had again commandeered boats, this time 'absolutely all boats', with their boatmen, all brought to 'Cotingelade', which was at that time the best available watercourse along which to bring his materials. As the water table in 1071 would have been considerably higher than it is now, the track from Belsar's Hill, then and later called the Mare's or mere's way, has to have been higher than the existing track to be at all usable, and the area around it would have been under water, although navigable by the flat-bottomed boats used in the Fens. The *Liber* stresses that the king was still trying to find a way to cross to the Isle, preferably by an unusual, that is an unexpected, route. The *Gesta* describes the king as constructing 'mounds and hillocks' by piling up his wood and other materials to make a platform on top of which his men might fight. This could have been located at the river's edge. He also built four round wooden towers from which he could use 'war machines' (*instrumentis praeliandi*), that is catapults and ballistae, to bombard the enemy. These fire javelins and rocks respectively. He was seeking to neutralise the peat defences built by the islanders.

The witch mounted the foremost of these towers and began her performance, beginning by 'denouncing destruction and uttering charms' together with other incantations intended to provoke the islanders. She is also reported to have bared her buttocks at the defenders, an early example of 'mooning', and this is reminiscent of the English defender at Exeter who dropped his britches (not unlike cropped jeans) to bare his genitals at the Normans, and then farted at them.

Hereward Counter-Attacks

Meanwhile Hereward had led his men silently and covertly into the area. He himself is described as mingling with the fishermen recruited by the king, as though urging them to greater efforts but perhaps warning them that a counterstroke was coming and that they should make themselves scarce. Then he threw off his disguise, donned his war gear and signalled his men to attack the enemy, their approach throwing the Norman ranks into confusion by setting fire to unused heaps of wood and to the piles of wood on which the towers stood and then the towers themselves, calling in English on God's help and praising him for his assistance. The whole structure rapidly went up in flames as the Normans fled in terror. As the *Liber Eliensis* puts it, 'a hundred men were routed from terror of one man and a thousand from confrontation with ten of his followers', that is, one Englishman was worth ten Frenchmen.

The witch, trapped on her burning tower, choking in the fumes and smoke, hysterical with fear 'as if by a whirlwind' fell headlong from the tower and broke her neck; so she who had intended to bring death to others had herself perished. The fire gradually grew fiercer, whipped up by the wind, and spread into the swamp of reeds for nearly two furlongs. This is how fire spreads in the Fens. The Norman soldiery, some on foot, others on horseback, fled along pathways in the marsh and on the beaten track and so rushed headlong into the marshes. Perhaps this was when William Malet died. The Normans were stupefied by the terrifying appearance of the raging fire and by the noise of burning as the willow branches crackled, almost driving them mad with fear. Hereward and his men pursued them, familiar as they were with their own district, ruthlessly slaying them from behind, firing arrows and throwing javelins, and so on this occasion scoring a great triumph.

So another great calamity had befallen the Normans who, in this account drawn from the *Gesta Herewardi* and *Liber Eliensis*, are depicted as suffering repeated defeats at Hereward's hands, though the author or authors cannot, in the end, disguise the fact that he was defeated. It may be that the effects of these successes have been exaggerated, since buried in the text of the *Liber* is an account, drawn possibly from the reminiscences of the garrison left at Ely after it was subdued, which, as will be seen, reports a version of the assault much more favourable to the Normans; it has the resistance brought to an end in a short and brutal assault by cavalry once the Norman army has, with the connivance of Abbot Thurstan, won its way onto the Isle.

The Final Phase

Before giving consideration to the final phase of the battle for Ely, with its accompanying implications not only of treachery and betrayal but of the use of deceit and misinformation by the king, some attention should be given to the waterborne aspects of the blockade. The *Liber Eliensis*, basing itself in part on Florence of Worcester's summary of events, asserts that the eastern side of the Isle was blockaded by water. King William used 'butsecarles', or fighting boatmen, to block all means of exit on that side so that not only were the defenders unable to escape by water, at least not in great numbers, but neither could they expect any more reinforcements such as Hereward had been receiving ever since he took refuge on the Isle, possibly as early as 1069.

Nor is it improbable that William would have been harrying the defences by sending in butsecarles to probe their strength. That there were such raids is rendered more probable by archaeological evidence. Eleventh-century weapons have been found in the river near Ely, at Braham Dock, at Dimmock's Cote, Wicken, and at Rolls or Rollers Lode where the roddam marks the original course of the Ouse; these weapons include spears and spear heads, axes and knives. None of this says anything about William's line of attack, but it does suggest a series of scattered raids. The *Liber Eliensis* and *Gesta Herewardi* do not pay any attention to this fighting, which military logic dictates must have occurred, because their accounts are concerned with the exploits of Hereward.

Although the text of the *Liber Eliensis* is strangely confused, seeking to connect events at Ely with the effects of the rebellion of the Norman Earls of Hereford and East Anglia in 1075 as well as looking back to the English Rising of 1069 (in which, it claims, Hereward himself was involved, acting with other nobles to unite the English and call upon the help of the Danes), and mentioning, among other matters, the great famine of 1070–71, it offers an explanation for this as the author, or perhaps compiler, admits to the use of many histories which he has combined 'in summary fashion' using 'brief and tiny extracts', while omitting 'things which are beyond belief', more fully recounted in Brother Richard of Ely's book about Hereward's deeds.

Abbot Thurstan's Betrayal

Having spent time padding out his account in this manner, the compiler finally returns to his main theme and relates a story of how Abbot Thurstan and his monks sought to win the king's favour and restore the fortunes of the monastery. They do this by advising the king on the best way of making a renewed offensive against Hereward. They assure the king that the people of Ely and the Isle will cease their resistance if Thurstan removes from them his own guidance and support. This perhaps explains why, after the fall of the Isle, the common people were not included in the king's vengeance.

But this was not the end of it. Orderic Vitalis has his own 'take' on the situation at Ely, because he sought to magnify the reputation of Earls Edwin and Morcar and to show off how ill-used they were by King William. He had already excused their rebellion of 1068 as provoked by 'envious and greedy' followers of the king and describes the brothers as 'zealous in the service of God ... remarkably handsome, nobly connected ... and well-loved by the people'. He then relates how Morcar and the other leading men, in Hereward's absence according to the *Liber*, were deceived into offering surrender. Orderic was himself either confused or misinformed about the exact sequence of events or preferred to dramatise the whole affair. His version affects to believe that Edwin was killed after rather than before the attack on Ely. This allows him to give a romantic flavour to the eventual death of Earl Edwin. The earl is said to have attempted either to free Morcar from his imprisonment or to avenge him. He is described as preferring death to life in his vain attempt and as having tried to persuade the Welsh, the Scots and the English, over a period of six months, to help him free his brother, only to be betrayed to the Normans by three of his own servants and killed while 'penned up beside a tidal stream' which prevented his escape. This is unsubstantiated and romantic. The period of six months 'on the run' refers to the time immediately before the arrival of the earls at Ely and after they escaped from William's custody at court. One point can be made here about the conviction of the accounts in the *Liber* and the *Gesta* that Edwin remained at Ely during the siege. It is known that Orderic visited the Fenland monasteries, including Ely, towards the end of the eleventh century, so perhaps it was his apparently convincing tale about Edwin and his insistence that he died after the fall of the Isle that led these authors to believe he remained at Ely.

More importantly, in his prelude to this tale, he says something much more credible and important. He alleges that King William, 'ill-advisedly relying on evil counsellors', damaged his own reputation by 'treacherously surrounding' Earl Morcar at Ely despite his being a man who had made peace with him. This is all part of his effort to blacken William's reputation (which includes a fierce denunciation of his harrying of the North). He then says that William sent 'crafty messengers proposing treacherous terms' to Morcar who were sent to tell him that if he were to surrender he would 'be received in peace as a loyal friend', which would be preferable to continuing to hold out, protected only by 'the inaccessibility of the place' which prevented him from slipping away by boat 'along the surrounding rivers to the sea'. Yet William had posted large numbers of butsecarles to prevent just such a manoeuvre.

Morcar, however, was deceived and surrendered, leading his men peacefully out of the island to seek the king. As a result he was thrown into jail in the charge of Roger, castellan of Beaumont, and ended his days as a prisoner.

The consequence of these stratagems employed by King William would seem to be that the earl and his men agreed not to contest the king's final, and successful, attack. It also seems probable that similar 'crafty messengers' visited Abbot Thurstan. But the *Liber*'s story is a complex one which begins by reviewing the 'evil things going on in the kingdom', such as the 'general takeover' of the resources of the churches which is confused with rumours that the king intended to confiscate the lands of Ely, driving the community, after prayers to heaven and appeals to 'Christ's beloved betrothed, Aethelthryth', into a decision to send envoys to King William, seeking mercy and peace. The claim that the conflict between Ely and the king lasted seven years is repeated. The *Gesta Herewardi* supports part of this story by emphasising William's decision to appropriate the lands of the Church of Ely that lay nearest to the Isle and divide them among his followers.

Arguments arose between the monks and the 'captains who guarded the city and the exit routes by water' who were probably Hereward's allies, with the monks threatening to go ahead with their plan to surrender and to hand over the lay defenders to the Normans. As this is not mentioned in the *Gesta*, it must come from a different source. This is part of the compiler's effort to exonerate the monks from any part in the resistance. Yet both the *Gesta* and the *Liber Eliensis* have them dining in full companionship with the soldiers and even going out on raids with them. It may be that there were two factions among the monks. The *Liber* account paints a picture of the defenders' despair and stresses their fear of the Normans. This would seem to come from a third source which might well be based on the anecdotes passed on by the Norman garrison.

The tale then is that Thurstan and his monks did a deal with King William. When the monks heard that church lands were actually being confiscated, they told Thurstan of this on his return from a visit in disguise to the hamlet of 'Angerhale' (in Bottisham), where he had hidden much of the Ely treasure and ornaments, and the community now decided to sue for peace. The text says this was done at Warwick, but that is actually where Thurstan later received a charter guaranteeing to the abbey that its possessions would be restored 'freely and honourably' after the struggle was over. Some of the text of the *Liber* uses the wording of that charter to add detail to its account. It is certainly describing how Thurstan had to humble himself to William to secure an agreement after paying the enormous fine levied on the monks for their defiance, but puts this too early in the account. The compiler endeavours to gloss over the humiliation of Thurstan by claiming that he drove a hard bargain, demanding that William could only be sure of obtaining entry onto the Isle if he first treated the monks well and guaranteed restoration of their lands and goods. William de Warenne and 'Gilbert of Clare' (probably Richard fitzGilbert) were to be guarantors of the king's promise. This again is surely part of the bargain at Warwick and not connected to the assistance rendered to William by the abbot. What is clear is that in order to win the king's clemency (Thurstan and the monks were not harmed, although they were heavily fined), the abbot explained to William how he could take successful counter-measures against the rebels and assured him that he, Thurstan, would ensure that the common folk, who depended on his 'guidance and support', would cease their resistance as their morale was poor in any case. It was arranged that William would be assisted in coming to the Isle secretly while Hereward and his men were away foraging for supplies. All this was concealed from Hereward.

As a result, William found it easy to plan his next move. He is described as making a progress around the kingdom (which relates to 1070) to 'fortify suitable places' so that he could 'thwart the forays of the rebels'. This is an example of the writer's 'double-vision' by which he conflates or confuses events which occurred during the great rebellion in 1069–70 with those of the Ely campaign. What William probably did was go out to ensure that those on the Isle could not escape him, strengthening the 'watch on the Isle', fully expecting that he would now be the winner. The vital point is that he is pictured as focussing his efforts on 'the place where he knew most of the enemy were to be found, namely Ely'. He again brings up siege engines, because Ely was well fortified, and 'laboured ... daily to take it by storm', something Cnut in his day had failed to achieve. Aldreth is nowhere mentioned in this version of his attack.

9

The Last Assault:
The King Victorious

Having devised a new approach, the king brought his men up from 'Cotingelade', here called '*lacus Cotingelade*', and led them on a laborious and winding march through the marshes, by a path revealed to him by the monks, and after reaching the river built a pontoon bridge based on a number of Fen boats. The advance this time was across generally marshy ground which would 'hardly support the footsteps of a man or any animal' and open to being targeted by archers. It is an area of streams and rivers where the ground is easily loosened by the slightest rain, characterised by beds of flag iris covering, and disguising, the marshy soil. The area was treacherous underfoot, liable in fine weather to split open into wide cracks. The weather was now turning harsh, the knights assailed by heavy rain mixed with hail which exhausted them so that they were ready to abandon the attack as they fought their way through the 'narrowings and windings' of the causeway or track through the marsh which cut men off from both sight and sound of each other, leaving each man anxious for his own safety at the expense of those ahead or behind. Some of the wording of this is borrowed from Orderic Vitalis's account of William's Pennine march, including the restlessness of the Bretons in his army, but can still be taken as reflecting the situation near Ely. (Medieval writers were prone to use quotations borrowed from other authors to express their own ideas, provided the text could be adapted sufficiently to their requirements.)

One grisly note is added. The men found themselves walking at times over the corpses of dead horses killed in the marshes, a macabre sort of bridge. This suggests that they were not far from the location of that first abortive attack after the king arrived at the Ouse from Cambridge via Reach at the opening of his campaign. William encouraged his men, briefly, by assuring them of the rewards which would follow a successful attack, and declared that he would carry on with it even if some were to give up. All this is new matter, not found in the *Gesta Herewardi* (which treats the actual end of the struggle very cursorily, not wanting to dwell on it), and casts a new light on William's success. William assured his men that the difficulties before them had to be overcome for the sake of the tranquillity of the kingdom.

At this point the *Liber* again abandons its source for another, and goes off at a tangent to discuss what 'Edwin and Morcar' were doing while Hereward was absent just before the king arrived at the Isle. They are credited with carrying out their own attacks on the Normans, going out by boat, and winning great booty in the process, storing it up against the day when the 8,000 exiles could be persuaded to return with the help of the Danes. The Norman manoeuvres up to that point are reviewed, including their approach to the Isle from Cotingelade, and William is said to have declared that he had no intention of wasting the efforts already made to put an end to the resistance of Ely.

This final attack is misleadingly described as a second attempt, so telescoping the two failures at Aldreth into one. But this time, as remarked earlier, a pontoon bridge is to be used. First he ensured that escape for the defenders would be well-nigh impossible, by taking full possession of the rivers 'with an armed fleet' (a further indication of the naval dimension to this struggle) and he himself, this time, stipulated that the marshes should be crossed by using pontoons (not a causeway), how the materials of which they were made were to be used and of what sort they should be. Work proceeded despite attackers from the Isle descending on them, killing a number of men and destroying part of the siege work. This only served to infuriate the king and his men even more. The *Liber* assures us that the Normans were now more hopeful of success because William had 'led the army unharmed right the way across, to a position nearer than anyone's expectation anticipated, to the waters of Ely'.

A quite detailed description of the area to be crossed is given. It is an area of 'numerous standing waters and fast flowing streams' which were a barrier to progress, and when the king reached 'the neighbourhood of the Isle' he encountered 'a marsh of horrific appearance, of infinite depth, festering all around to the depths of its hollow bed'. Study of maps reconstructing the now long-dried-up waterways around Ely and the Isle suggests that there were few, if any, streams flowing into the Old West River at Aldreth and therefore the location of this attack needs to be sought elsewhere.

William struggled to make progress through the marshes in person in order to encourage his men by example. This rings true as an example of the Conqueror's character, as he had behaved in this manner on other occasions. At one point he is even said to have waded through some river in which he was submerged almost to the top of his helmet. At last, as a reference to 'the opposite bank' indicates, he reached the main river where he found his enemies entrenched behind peat blocks, ready to bar the way to the Normans with stones and missiles. The double obstacle of a river and defensive works disconcerted the Normans, who might well have been relying on Thurstan's guidance to bring them unopposed onto the Isle.

The king was no whit disturbed. He ordered little boats to be brought there, through the Fen, from which a pontoon bridge was constructed on top of them by means of poles and wicker hurdles and then, by 'an amazing feat of engineering' which cost great effort, he had siege engines erected on the river bank with which to bombard the defences. As soon as these were ready, the 'softening up' began and so tremendous was the barrage – of all sorts of projectiles fired by catapults and ballistae – that 'the unstable ground shook, threatening everyone supported by it with drowning'. It is possible that, as hinted at by the *Liber* and the *Gesta*, which talk of seven days of fighting, in fact this softening-up process took several days.

Eventually bombardment was stopped because 'the wretched men gave way' and fled. Led by the king himself, the Norman knights and footsoldiers swarmed across this 'weak and shaky bridge'. Even after making the crossing, the men still had to contend with pools of water and found it difficult to struggle onto solid ground through 'pitfalls and eddies of mud'. The Norman force consisted of a thousand French knights in body-armour and helmets, and they now joined battle against three thousand of the 'pirates' and greater numbers of English militia, who had been brought there from 'the Midlands' (meaning, perhaps, the central areas of the Isle as well as men from further afield), as well as many of the common people of the Isle. Then, as the source used by the *Liber Eliensis* has it:

> Then a resounding cry of victory drove the enemy with high speed from the Isle. The Normans, flaring up and surrounding some thousands, in a moment destroyed them, so that few escaped and they only with difficulty.

Naturally, the *Liber* claims that the defenders fled at the very sight of King William, 'this amazing and terrible warrior', as he went into action with his men, attacking and striking the enemy down with great boldness. The account concludes at this point with a eulogy of the Conqueror, partially derived from William of Poitiers' *Gesta Guillelmi*. It is this passage which also recalls the Aeneid and the Thebaid.

The affair was not yet over. William still had to take possession of Ely itself and deal with those he regarded as the ringleaders. His army had now entered the Isle but the march to Ely was still not easy, requiring more riding and marching along the 'crooked fenpaths' in order to ambush and enforce the surrender of the rest of the enemy. Nonetheless, this was soon accomplished, especially as Morcar, according to Orderic Vitalis, had already decided to trust the king and make his submission. The *Gesta* version tells us little of the aftermath because its concern is with Hereward, but the *Liber Eliensis* is graphic in its description of the fate of those who surrendered:

> The armed men were led out: first the leaders, then a considerable number of men who were prominent because of their reputation or some mark of distinction. He sentenced some to imprisonment, some to the loss of eyes, hands or feet; he released unpunished the mass of common people.

Confiscation of the plentiful goods he found there compensated the king for the horses that had been killed and the inconvenience to which he had been put.

The confusion in the sources which left the compiler of the *Liber* to believe in the presence of Earl Edwin continued up to the end. Basing himself on a source which might ultimately derive from Orderic Vitalis, he believed that Edwin, not Morcar, was captured and that

Morcar escaped. In part this is a confused and inverted version of Orderic's notion that Edwin was still alive after the siege and tried to rescue Morcar. But it might also be that the original source mentioned no names, talking only of leaders or earls, and that the wrong names were inserted. The most remarkable point supporting this is an obvious one. The last sentence of this paragraph in the *Liber* reads:

> Morcar himself, and a few men, escaped with difficulty.

Compare this with the statements in Florence of Worcester:

> Hereward ... with a few others made his escape through the Fens.

and Gaimar:

> Hereward ... he escaped with a few men.

The *Peterborough Chronicle* says the nobles surrendered 'excepting only Hereward' and 'they who would go with him'.

Perhaps the *Liber* should read 'Morcar was taken captive ... Hereward, himself, and a few men, escaped with difficulty.' A few words could easily have been omitted.

An Odd Story

William now behaved very curiously; he had guards posted at the entrances to the church, so that he would not be importuned by the monks coming out in procession with crosses and saints' relics while he prayed. He is said to have been a conventionally pious man and so perhaps feared that they would prevail upon him to be merciful because he could not, in terms of fairness, have remained unmoved and so would lose the moral high ground which would allow him to punish them.

He entered the church but did not dare approach too near the tomb containing the body of the holy virgin, Etheldreda (Aethelthryth), but instead threw a gold mark onto the altar, fearing the judgement God might pass on him for the evils perpetrated by his men in capturing the holy sanctuary. 'Gilbert of Clare', finding the monks dining in their refectory, then scolded them, as 'wretched and deluded men' who preferred to eat rather than take note that the king was visiting them and was at that moment in the church, and this despite William having left guards to keep them out of it. They hurriedly ran to the church only to find it still guarded and the king gone.

They then persuaded Gilbert to intercede on their behalf with the king who had withdrawn from his agreement with them because of their behaviour. Gilbert did as he was asked and persuaded William to meet a delegation of monks at Witchford. He there agreed to grant them his favour once more in return for a payment of 700 silver marks. They were forced to take a large quantity of church treasure, crosses, altar decorations, reliquaries, woven fabrics, and church plate of all kinds, chalices, patens, bowls etc., in order to find the money which was to be handed over at Cambridge. There, owing to a 'trick on the part of the moneyers' the amount was found to be one eighth of an ounce short, whereupon the king affected to be extremely angry and used this as an excuse to withhold his peace still until they had appeased his wrath with a further payment of 300 marks, making 1,000 in all.

This finally secured for Ely restoration to the king's favour and possession of its liberties and estates. That was only done, of course, by surrendering everything else of value in the church and even the image of the Virgin Mary with the infant Jesus 'seated on a throne of marvellous workmanship' (that is 'Our Lady of Ely'), which Abbot Aelfsine had had made of gold and silver. They also had to strip the images of St Aethelthryth and her sisters of their ornaments. As William was described, when safely dead, as 'sunk in greed and utterly given up to avarice' (*Peterborough Chronicle* 1086) this story certainly rings true.

Abbot Thurstan is said to have then begun a campaign to recover Ely's lands from those who had appropriated them. Those who proved recalcitrant and unwilling to come to terms with him were placed under an anathema, solemnly cursed by bell, book and candle, and any who seized abbey lands thereafter, together with their descendants, were similarly cursed. The monks were in no doubt that his curses were effective.

Locating the Final Attack

Thus ended the siege of Ely and its immediate aftermath. But a major question is as yet unanswered and that is a conundrum. Where, exactly, did William make that final, deadly assault? If the account in the *Liber Eliensis*, which contains much matter towards the end of its account of the siege which is not to be found in the *Gesta Herewardi*, is carefully examined, it will be noted that nowhere does it say that this final attack was launched at Aldreth. Quite the reverse, because it maintains that William moved 'towards the place where he knew most of the enemy were to be found, namely, Ely'. There he laboured to cross much marshy ground, using a way with many 'windings and narrowings' despite a multitude of difficulties and brought his army 'unharmed right the way across, to a position nearer than anyone's expectation anticipated, to the waters of Ely'. This cannot be Aldreth, which is fully seven miles from Ely. He also appears to be using an existing causeway, literally a way through the marshes used by the inhabitants of the Fens and, presumably, revealed to him by Abbot Thurstan and his monks. He was thus enabled to move his army, complete with cavalry, across the Cotingelade lake (*lacus Cotingelade*) by means of flat-bottomed Fenland boats and approach Ely by way of the marshes.

This time the king did not build a causeway. He had the marshland 'bridged with pontoons', that is he was using the flat-bottomed 'canoes' of the region. The *Liber* states plainly that he 'had little boats transported there through the fen'. Examples of the sort of boats most likely to have been used have been found. Several were found at the deepening of the river at Wisbech, at Deeping Fen, at Haddenham and even at Denver sluice. The 'canoe-boat' found at Deeping Fen was made from a single tree. It was some 40 feet long and 5 feet 8 inches at its stern. Other examples were smaller, averaging 2 feet 4 inches in width with sides less than 6 inches high and flat-bottomed; floating platforms. They are the forerunners of today's punts.

The king used boats of similar construction to carry siege engines, ballistae and catapults with which to bombard the opposition. He had already successfully crossed the Channel and brought horses with him. As he used cavalry in the final stages of this battle, he probably used these 'pontoons' (punts) to transport men and horses through the marshes and then finally bridged the river which barred his way to the higher ground, upon which Ely could be seen, by making a pontoon bridge. This was constructed of these same little boats with poles and wicker hurdles laid across them. A barrage of missiles was laid down, possibly repeated over several days, and then his 'one thousand French Knights' crossed over and joined battle with the enemy.

No real resistance was offered by the by now leaderless English. Morcar and the notables surrendered, trusting in false promises, and Hereward was apparently absent. The defenders were surrounded and made prisoner. The Normans rapidly occupied both the town and the abbey and William, after a cursory visit, set up camp at Witchford. So, where did this take place?

Both geography and topography are against Aldreth; it is simply too far away and was, in any case, already the scene of two major disasters. To attack a third time at that location is militarily improbable. It can also be suggested that the terrain at Aldreth was no longer available to the king. In his destruction of the king's siege towers, Hereward not only set fire to the towers, but he also fired the sedge. As a result the marshes themselves, and the underlying peat, caught fire. Peat fires are almost impossible to extinguish. They continue to burn even below the surface waters and fire travels out of sight for very many metres. Men could be killed falling into burning pits. The area around the Aldreth river bank would have been too dangerous to be used again as a base for an attack. In any case, Abbot Thurstan had offered an alternative route which would bring the king much nearer to Ely. The causeway at Aldreth seems too straight to fit the description 'winding and narrowing' and the Fen there was nearer sixteen than four furlongs in width.

An alternative site was suggested by T. C. Lethbridge in the 1930s, and that is Stuntney. Although it does bring William much nearer to Ely, it cannot be accepted. The 'ancient' causeway there is Bronze Age and in the wrong area. Furthermore, the river was, in the eleventh century, in the wrong place. It ran along in front of the island, as it was, of Stuntney, towards Prickwillow. Its course today is marked by a rodham (or roddon) and a narrow watercourse, and reaches Prickwillow by way of Rollers or Roll's Lode. It is approximately a mile from Stuntney to where the river now runs so that, in William's day, he would have had to cross another mile of swamp after crossing the river and would have been under constant attack from the higher ground beyond. His siege engines could not have fired successfully across such a distance. Stuntney as an option can safely be dismissed. This does not preclude the possibility of waterborne attacks from Stuntney and, indeed, all along the eastern edge of the Isle. These would have kept the defenders constantly busy and uncertain where the next attack might arise. It is also worth noting that, after his escape, Hereward is said to have stationed two men on Stuntney to make a diversion. It cannot therefore have been in Norman occupation.

It is, perhaps, important to stress that William was unlikely to have relied at any time on one single point of attack. The strategy would have been, as in all medieval sieges, to exhaust the defending garrison by means of constant alarms and excursions. William had not recruited butsecarles and brought ships up the Ouse on the eastern side for them to sit and do nothing. The sources, both the *Gesta* and the *Liber*, are concerned mainly to inform us of the deeds of Hereward, and their accounts naturally stress the fighting in which he was involved. The *Liber*, also, was much concerned with the attacks conducted by the king in person. Little or nothing is known about any attacks made by the king's barons, but they must certainly have launched their own forays. Equally, nothing is said of any fighting involving Earl Morcar and his men or led by Siward Barn, but this does not mean that they did nothing.

In the eleventh century, the Cam, then called Granta or '*Gronte fluminis*', flowed down through Stretham towards Ely, reinforced by a number of tributaries, especially the East River or Estee which originated in the same watershed as the Westee or Old West River (which flowed west past Aldreth to join the Ouse near Earith) and then swung east towards and in front of Stuntney. Where it flowed east and then north past Ely it was called the

Prickwillow Ouse. At some point between Braham Dock and Little Thetford other little streams flowed into the river, one of which was known as the Alderbrook and near it, too, lay the Alderforth or Ford. Both names are indicative that this area, like Aldreth, was noted for its alders. It would appear that in the thirteenth century, as records show, the stretch of river between, approximately, Braham Farm and Little Thetford, was called 'Hereward's Reach' (a specific stretch of a river) and somewhere there also was 'Hereward's Beach', all according to thirteenth- and fourteenth-century records. It is also the case that to some the remains of a Roman Fort at Braham Farm were called Hereward's Fort. Nearby again was the Alderforde, that is alor-ford, a name also found in thirteenth-century documents. It lay between Little Thetford and Braham Farm, where the marsh and river crossing were about four furlongs wide. The Alderbrook was in the same area. All of this suggests a folk memory of an association between this part of the river and Hereward's defence of Ely.

Although most interpretations of the names given to the location of King William's attacks, that is Alrehede, Alrehethe etc., accept this as 'Alor-hythe' or landing place of the Alders, and so identify the location as Aldreth near Haddenham, there are two places in the *Gesta* where the location is given, according to several transcribers, as Aldereche or 'Alor-reach' a stretch of river where the alders grow. This could as easily refer to a stretch of the river below Stretham as to one at Aldreth. It could also mean 'Ald' or Old-reach. But a close inspection of the original text of the *Gesta Herewardi*, part of Richard of Swaffham's Register, now Manuscript 1 of the Peterborough Archives and deposited in Cambridge University Library, reveals that the reading is clearly *ALREHETHE* (it occurs twice), just as the earlier references to Aldreth read *ALREHEDE*. Both mean 'landing stage of the alders'.

In the *Liber Eliensis* (Section 110) a final account of

the taking of Ely is given, probably derived from the memories of the Norman Garrison left in occupation after the surrender. This begins with a crossing of a 'lake called Cotingelade' in response to daily attacks throughout the area by Hereward and his men. The king 'took possession of the rivers with an armed fleet' and 'bridged the marshland ... with pontoons' and so 'came eventually into the neighbourhood of the Isle' where he was first confronted by a 'marsh of horrific appearance, infinite depth, festering all around to the depths of its hollow bed'. He pressed on against enemy attacks using little boats to transport his siege engines, bombarded his opponents into retreat and then led the army across the marsh and river by means of a pontoon bridge. Thus he entered the Isle and forced the surrender of his foes following a most difficult march. Only one location fits the context of this account and it is not Aldreth, which was not approached by nor anywhere near a marsh of infinite depth. It is worth commenting here that William's tactics at Ely echo those he used in his crossing of the River Aire on his way north to deal with the uprising of 1069. There he was confronted by a river he could not cross, there were no bridges he could use and the current was too fast. He was delayed for three weeks until his scouts had discovered a ford, perhaps after the waters had gone down somewhat. There he used a bombardment by ballista to cover his advance and forced the ford, causing the opposing Danes to retreat and take refuge with their fleet, thus providing adequate precedent for the tactics now used at Ely.

In his book *Merlin's Island*, T. C. Lethbridge talks about the area around Fordy Farm opposite Little Thetford (once known as Piuteforde or the people's Ford and also as Theo-ford; the ford of the nation), known in some sources as Chapel Hill (indicating an area of relatively higher ground). Here there might have been a hermitage on this rise, then an islet, for a recluse who kept open the ford and the trackway leading to it. It stands on a finger of clay and gravel which is an extension of the Wicken Peninsula. In this area the river, from Little Thetford down to Braham Dock, has given up battleaxes, spears and spear hafts similar to those illustrated in the Bayeux Tapestry. In 1924 workmen dredging the river at Braham Dock found several spearheads of eleventh-century style (and some human bones). Little or nothing of the appropriate date has been found at Aldreth. In that area and to the south as far as Willingham finds have been of bronze rather than iron. Weapons have also been found at various places to the east and south-east of the Little Thetford area, for instance, in Burwell Fen and at Dimmock's Cote on the Cam, at Wicken and at Quaveney, notably spears, axes and a scramasax. Spears are rarely found in East Anglia except in Cambridgeshire and the Fens. Some have the kind of sockets which indicate continental, perhaps French, origin. These finds illustrate that this whole eastern area was probably the scene of much fighting, though they do not reveal the Conqueror's actual line of approach.

It is true that the main route from Cambridge to Ely was the way via Arbury Camp along the 'King's Highway' to Belsar's Hill and so to the Ouse (not the West River), but this brings the traveller to Stretham, and not far from there the Roman Car Dyke, much neglected in the eleventh century, met the Cam and archaeologists accept that the Dyke linked the Cam and the Ouse. At that point parts of two swords have been found, and a shield boss and spear as well as several human skulls, all of the right period. Some way down river lay Little Thetford, and it was from there to Braham Farm nearby that the smallest gap in the Fen was to be found, the most likely site for a crossing. Opposite Little Thetford lay Reed Fen. The distance to Ely from here is less than 2 km and to Witchford just over 2 km. Archaeologists believe that more than one causeway was built south of Ely when William besieged Hereward, and not on the west which could only be approached by water. Perhaps the insistence in the sources that William attacked from the west is to be explained by the idea that his final attack took place on a stretch of water which, by the twelfth century, was known as West Water or Westee, that is the Old West River.

It can now be argued that King William, informed by Abbot Thurstan of Hereward's absence, and learning from the same source about the ancient trackway leading to Fordy and the ford at Little Thetford, withdrew his forces from the vicinity of Aldreth, where he had already suffered two embarrassing defeats, transported men and horses by means of pontoons, that is flat-bottomed boats, and swung around in an arc, via the Cam, to reach this 'narrow and winding path' and so struggled through the marshes, arriving perhaps at the edges of the great mere (now long extinct) called 'Harrimere' or 'Averingemere', where it would have been well-nigh impossible to discern which was mere and which was river. Bypassing the mere he would have arrived at the banks of the Ouse and from Church Hill proceeded to bombard into submission those defenders who presumed to bar his way. Having pulverised the opposition, he constructed a 'weak and shaky bridge' of linked pontoons overlain with hurdles and reeds, perhaps even sinking the boats into the ford, and so enabled his knights to sweep triumphantly onto the Isle where they could ride over the higher ground between Little Thetford and Ely, a distance of under 2 km. Some might well have swung past what is now Grunty Fen, while others followed what was left of Akeman Street, so surrounding and enforcing the surrender of the defenders who, in the absence of Hereward and let down by the decision of Morcar and the other notables to trust William's promises, without leadership simply surrendered.

The decision to use waterborne transport for much of the way would have been crucial. That he used the Cam suggests that the Car Dyke was used also. That would also explain the references to 'lake Cotingelade' in the text, since the Car Dyke seems to have run from 'Beche' (Landbeach) to Chare Fen in Cottenham and from there to the Ouse and Harrimere. That latter place might well be the 'marsh of horrific appearance and of infinite depth' which barred his way. So William went 'around the crooked fen paths in a most difficult march', reaching the Isle by 'an unusual route'. Thus he came to Little Thetford, where the distance from one piece of solid ground to the next is consistent with the texts. It also matches Florence's eastern beach, '*orientali plaga*', a phrase used by the *Liber Eliensis*.

The area to the east of Chapel Hill would have been 'brown' rather than 'green' fen. The green fen was firm ground, suitable for horses, and that is what William found after crossing at Little Thetford. The brown fen, of peat and deep fen, was watered by '*eaus*' or river reaches and by meres and covered in sedge grass. Little Thetford itself contains a low, sand-capped hill near Bedwell Hay Farm, just about a mile south of Ely. This little hill fits the idea of a 'dun' and there is a Saxon site at this location which some archaeologists suggest may be the famous 'Cratendune', the inhabitants of which St Etheldreda had removed to the higher ground around her church and abbey. The Saxon cemetery, probably belonging to this village, consisting of some thirty inhumation graves, lies quite nearby. It was found when the area was flattened for Witchford Aerodrome (Second World War bomber station) revealing plentiful objects of the fifth to the seventh century. A magnificent pendant with Christian motifs which could have been the property of a royal personage was found in 1952.

There had been much confusion over the events at Ely, caused by the degree of attention paid to Aldreth. This certainly appears to have been William's early choice, but he failed twice there and preferred, as the *Liber Eliensis* makes clear, a route suggested by Abbot Thurstan. Aldreth attracts attention because later in the twelfth century and after, it was the main way onto the Isle. Some sources insist that it was the work of Bishop Hervey rather than the Conqueror. In all likelihood the Bishop reinstated a route previously built by order of the Conqueror, as his writ of 1082 confirms. But it would have needed a solid bridge in order to be of any use and that must have been built after both the Isle and Ely town had been subdued. Even after Hervey's time it was not always maintained, and King Stephen (*Gesta Stephani* 62) found it necessary to imitate the Conqueror's tactic when he came to Ely to drive out Bishop Nigel, a supporter of the Empress Matilda, who had fortified Ely against him. Stephen found the route from Belsar's Hill, where it began from a junction of several ancient tracks, narrow and winding, and at Aldreth he had to use a pontoon bridge to get his men across the river, so the bridge must have been neglected also.

It was, perhaps, Stephen's decision to cross at Aldreth, where he found a '*castellulum*' guarding the crossing, and to use a pontoon bridge, which fixed Aldreth in people's minds as the location of William's crossing also. Current opinion is that this 'little castle' was probably at Belsar's Hill. There would have been no solid ground available at the river. '*Castellum*' refers not to a castle as such but to the palisade (with or without a ditch and bank) surrounding the motte and the bailey and such palisades could be used without the construction of a motte or mound and its tower or donjon.

10

Hereward after Ely:
The Enigma of his Ultimate Fate

With the fall of Ely and the submission of the defenders to King William, the *Liber Eliensis* loses all interest in the doings of Hereward. The sole sources for what happened next are thus the *Gesta Herewardi*, which returns to the text of 'Leofric the Deacon', and Geoffrey Gaimar, who has much more to say about Hereward's activities after he fled from Ely than about his actions while he was there. But the sad fact is that these two sources flatly contradict each other and cannot be reconciled. This has disposed most historians to throw in the towel and simply say something to the effect that Hereward now moves out of history into myth. This is rather cavalier.

A better approach is to examine what these two sources (and the somewhat suspect fourteenth-century writer Ingulf) have to say and attempt to decide between them, or even arrive at a third possibility. If this is to be done, then Gaimar's account should be taken first, partly because it has been suggested that his version is the earliest we have apart from the entries in the chronicle, which say only that Hereward escaped from Ely and are silent about his fate.

Gaimar's Account

This is part of his 'L'Estorie des Engles', written about

1138–39 in medieval French verse, and owing much to his acquaintance with Geoffrey of Monmouth's *Historia Britonum*. Geoffrey based his work on a now lost version of the *Old English Chronicle*, which he calls the 'Book of Wassingburc' (Washingborough) and on a copy of the 'little book belonging to the Archdeacon of Oxford' which was also used by Monmouth. Gaimar's work contains a mixture of history and fable and it is not always clear which is which. He was writing for his patroness, Constance, wife of a minor Lincolnshire baron, Ralph fitzGilbert. These two had influential friends such as the great Yorkshire baron Walter l'Espec and may have been members of the fitzGilbert clan. So 'L'Estorie des Engles' was intended both for private reading and for public recitation by the author as an entertainment at feasts and banquets.

Gaimar's account of Hereward makes him '*un des meillures del région*' or one of the most noble men in the country, and yet a leader of men who are 'outlaws to King William'. He and his men join forces with Earl Morcar and other leading Englishmen at 'Welle', the area between Outwell and Upwell, and they all go to Ely intending to remain there over winter and then go into exile, probably in Flanders. But the king, on learning of their presence in Ely, decides to act against them, summons both land- and ship-borne forces, besieges the Isle of Ely and makes a bridge (not a causeway) to gain access to the Isle, whereupon everyone save Hereward surrenders.

He, with a few others, seven in all including a relative called Geri, escape through the reeds in a boat. They kill astonishing numbers of both Normans and Englishmen who are with them, steal horses and take refuge by way of Huntingdon in the forest of Brunneswald. Up to this point Gaimar agrees with the *Gesta*. There is now, as pointed out earlier, a major disagreement with the accounts in the chronicle. Gaimar claims that Hereward now attacks Peterborough and also Stamford, which drives him off although he is supposed to have a force of 700 men. This is a misplaced version of his assault in league with the Danes which the major sources insist took place before the siege of Ely and the departure of the Danes in 1070. It is curious that Gaimar and the *Gesta* agree on a raid on Peterborough after the affair at Ely. This suggests that they drew on a common source or tradition. Gaimar also agrees with Hugh Candidus in talking of an attack on Stamford, although Hugh involves Abbot Turold in this fight and even has him captured by Hereward's men and ransomed for an impossibly large sum. It is not impossible, in view of these coincidences, that Hereward's band was involved in fighting in and around both Peterborough and Stamford and that those skirmishes in time became confused with the earlier and much more significant attack by Hereward and the Danes.

Another point of contact between Gaimar and the *Gesta* is the role of the Lady Alftrude or Aelfthryth. The *Gesta* has a reference to the 'wife of Earl Dolfin' who agrees to intercede for Hereward so that he can be reconciled to King William. Gaimar names the lady who intercedes on his behalf as Alftrude and then asserts that Hereward married her. The *Gesta* carefully claims that his Flemish wife Turfrida was now a nun at Crowland and that Hereward had repudiated her. This claim reappears in the *History of Crowland* by Ingulf. If Alftrude (that is, Aelfthryth) was the '*uxor*', wife or widow, of an 'Earl Dolfin', can this be substantiated? There might, in fact, have been such a person. Cospatrick I Earl of Dunbar (previously Earl of Northumbria) had three sons. His youngest, Cospatrick II, eventually succeeded him and died at the battle of the Standard in 1138. The second son, Waltheof, eventually became a monk at Crowland

and was abbot from 1126 to 1138, according to Orderic Vitalis. (That might explain the tradition at Crowland.) The eldest son was called Dolfin, of whom we know only that he was driven out of Cumbria by William Rufus. Curiously, Cospatrick II was never styled 'earl', which suggests the possibility that his elder brother was indeed 'Earl Dolfin' and that he was, as the eldest, a married man. If he had been injured in some way or otherwise become incapable of fulfilling his role as earl, perhaps his wife did leave him for someone else, and that someone was Hereward. This is quite speculative, but does explain the links at Crowland between Hereward, Turfrida and 'Earl' Dolfin's wife. All other information about Turfrida is found only in Ingulf's *History*.

Beyond this point Gaimar and the *Gesta* part company. Gaimar knew of the assertion in the chronicle that when King William went to the war in Maine he took an English contingent with him:

> King William led an English army and a French oversea and won the district of Maine, and the English laid it completely waste; they destroyed the vineyards, burnt down the towns, completely devastated the countryside and brought it all onto subjection to William.

He therefore asserts that Hereward intended to go overseas to fight the people of Le Mans who had taken several castles from the king. He also says that he had been there on a previous occasion and that he had slain 'Gauter del Bois' and imprisoned 'Lord Geoffrey del Maine' for a week. This probably refers to Geoffrey of Mayenne, chief supporter of Azo of Liguria, son-in-law of the famous count Herbert 'Wake-dog', summoned from Italy by the rebels against King William back in 1069. Azo went back to Italy, convinced they only wanted his money, and the men of Le Mans drove out their rulers and set up a commune. William then intervened and devastated the area, forcing their surrender.

Gaimar says of Hereward that he had been to Le Mans on a previous occasion when the inhabitants had taken several castles from King/Duke William. Hereward is credited with killing 'Gauter del Bois' and keeping 'Lord Geoffrey del Maine' in prison for a week. (Lord Geoffrey identified above.) He held the castle of Mayenne south of Domfront which William took from him in 1064. The story goes that he was besieged by William for several days but that the Duke intended to waste little time in dealing with him and resorted to an underhand ruse. Unable to reach the castle by means of catapults or ballistae, because of its great height above ground level, he persuaded two children to seek entry into the castle, which they successfully did, and to set fire to the wooden structures behind the ramparts, so disrupting the defence and enabling William to seize the castle. Certainly Geoffrey of Mayenne had been effectively 'imprisoned' in his own castle for about a week. While it cannot be said that Hereward had anything to do with this affair, it is possible that he was serving in the Duke's army as a mercenary. Even if he was not, the story does suggest the source of Gaimar's assertion about him. The *Gesta Herewardi* has Hereward take part in early versions of tournaments at both Bruges in Flanders and much further south at Poitiers.

Similarly, there is a possible source for the tale about Gauter (Gautier) del Bois. After the end of William's siege of Le Mans and its surrender to him, the local inhabitants chose a certain Gautier de Mantes as their count. He had long been threatened by William with the loss of Mantes, a vulnerable frontier castle on the Seine. Gautier accepted the Norman victory and gave up his newly acquired county. The sources say that he and his wife Biota died shortly afterwards, possibly at Falaise as unwilling guests of the Duke. It was then rumoured that they had been poisoned at William's behest, but Orderic Vitalis states that it was at the hands of their enemies. It is just possible that this Gautier is Gaimar's Gauter del Bois and that he has borrowed the story of his death and attributed it to Hereward.

Gaimar gives a detailed account of an attack on Hereward by a band of jealous Normans who come upon him unawares while he is dining. They wait until he falls asleep and then attack him. Thus he is taken by surprise and unarmed. His weapons are those of a twelfth-century knight; he has a warhorse, hauberk, lance, sword and shield, and javelins. The fight is described at length and he kills at least eight men including 'Ralf de Dol', but, outnumbered as he is, he is sorely wounded. In his fight with Ralf, both are mortally wounded and die. Someone called Halselin, or Alselin, takes Hereward's head ('de Ereward le chef en prist', 'le chef' here literally meaning 'the head') probably cutting it off, and swears that had the English had three men like him the French would have been driven out of England.

As it is unlikely that Gaimar had access to an eyewitness account, the conclusion must be that the poet is giving his hero a truly heroic end. Gaimar's account is supported by no other source nor even referred to elsewhere, whereas the account given in the *Gesta*, unsatisfactory though it is in many respects, could be somewhat closer to the facts, as an account in very similar terms appears to lie behind the version of events given by the Pseudo-Ingulf. Only the *Liber de Hyda*, or *Chronicle of Hyde Abbey*, appears to follow Gaimar's view by claiming that in the end Hereward and all his men were killed. This is second hand and unreliable.

That Gaimar is not always relating verifiable history is indicated by his comment when reporting King William's war against King Malcolm in 1072 that these events are 'as the true history tells us'. Later he says he has 'inserted the accounts which the Welsh left out', out of the *Historia Britonum*, that is, and that he writes 'verses concerning the most noble deeds'.

The *Gesta Herewardi*

This account of Hereward's later activities differs entirely from Gaimar. It contains tales about Hereward with a supernatural flavour and a long and involved account of plots made against him by his Norman enemies after he has, as in Gaimar, been reconciled to King William through the intercession of the Lady Alftrude. These plots lead to his imprisonment, from which he escapes, and, through the mediation of his gaoler, called Robert de Horepol, he is again reconciled to the king and is restored to his family lands. He lives a long, peaceful life in the king's service:

> Thus Hereward the famous fighter ... was received into favour by the king and with his father's lands and possessions lived afterwards for many years, faithfully serving King William.

Ingulf adds that he 'ended his days in peace and was very recently, by his especial choice, buried in our monastery by the side of his wife'. Hereward's burial at Crowland was evidently by then a long-standing tradition of the monastery.

The opening stages of the *Gesta* account could well contain a kernel of fact. After meeting 'Alwin son of Ordgar', who persuades him not to set fire to the town and the abbey because it is already too late as the king is at Witchford and the Isle has fallen, Hereward slips away into the marshes, going north towards 'the sea called Wide near Welle', that is the Wash (which one source calls 'the Norman Sea') which at that time came much further inland than it does now, as far as Wisbech. There were ample channels through which he might effect his escape. As a delaying tactic, Hereward sends some of his men '*cis Saham*', that is to an area 'this side' of Soham and in fact to the island of Stuntney (*Stunteneia* not *Stimtencia* as in some transcriptions). They are to signal him by lighting fires and laying waste the area and then rejoin him. The intention was to mislead the Normans into looking for Hereward to the east rather than the north.

The outlaws are then pursued into the Brunneswald, in the 'great woods of Northamptonshire', by 'all the king's men' gathered from nine shires, although only seven are named, and they search the woods near Bourne. According to the *Gesta*, Abbot Turold and Ivo Taillebois lead the search but Hereward turns the tables on them by means of an ambush in which five Normans of great importance are captured including Turold (or, according to 'Ingulf', Ivo Taillebois). The *Gesta* then claims that the abbot and his nephew (he is known to have had at least two) and the others are ransomed for the impossible sum of £30,000 (something like 30 or even 300 silver marks might be believable). This would appear to be twelfth-century embroidery, as that was the convention of war between nobles and knights by that time, but not in Hereward's era.

If there is truth in this, it may be that these 'captives' were briefly surrounded and either fought their way out or Hereward decided that it was not feasible to hold them and let them go. This incident is not without corroboration of a kind. The *Annales Burgo-Spaldenses* (or *Chronicle of Abbot John*) says that Turold rewarded the knights in his service with fiefs because they had protected or defended him against Hereward but that nevertheless he and other 'magnates' had been captured and ransomed for 30,000 marks of silver, an equally improbable sum which again would have been credible as 30 or 300 marks. Walter of Whittlesey's additions to Hugh Candidus confirm that Turold gave fiefs to his knights, and Hugh himself maintains that the abbot distributed fiefs (manors held by military or other honourable services) to his relatives and his knights, and enfeoffed 'Geoffrey Infans' the abbot's nephew. The *Gesta* puts this in context by stating that Turold granted lands to his soldiers on condition that they gave him military assistance to subdue Hereward. They were to attack Hereward as their service for their lands.

It is possible that this tale belongs rather to the period between Hereward's attack on Peterborough, in company with the Danes, and the arrival at Ely of Morcar and his associates, that is to the year 1070. If so, that would explain why the next section of the *Gesta*, like Gaimar, puts the burning of Peterborough at this point, after rather than before the siege of Ely. This leads the writer to relate how, in a dream, Hereward has a vision of a man of 'indescribable form, of old and terrible aspect ... with a great key', which is clearly meant to be St Peter, the patron of the abbey, who threatens Hereward and orders him to restore its belongings to 'his church' or face a miserable death. The monks had surely devised this story as a means of showing how St Peter was wont to defend his abbey, just as at Ely there are the claims that St Etheldreda appeared to Gervase, the Steward of Picot, Norman Sheriff of Cambridgeshire, and struck him with her crozier (so, apparently, causing his death) for daring to extort money from the monks, and again how she caused Bishop Nigel's stone castle to fall down. It was also an explanation for the return of some of the Abbey's relics.

More wonders ensue. Hereward is guided through the marshes by a huge white dog, which turns out to be a wolf, and by burning flames which attach themselves to his soldiers' lances, '*which the common people call Faeries' lights*' (probably an effect of marsh gas). All this is, of course, romantic embroidery. The outlaws attack Stamford, and are repulsed by the citizens. As this shows them in an unfavourable light there is probably an element of truth in it. Hereward and his men meet and defeat various opponents, rather in the manner so familiar from the *Tales of Robin Hood*, of which character Hereward in the Brunneswald is a forerunner. He fights and defeats a 'Saxon soldier' called Letoltus and finally, after the intervention of the 'wife of Earl Dolfin', is reconciled to the king, while his Flemish wife Turfrida retires to become a nun at Crowland.

While at court he is challenged and insulted by '*Ogger*' (perhaps Ogier the Breton) and defeats him and this gives his enemies among the courtiers the pretext to give King William false and slanderous reports about him, accusing him of treachery to the kingdom. They insist on his being punished and he is imprisoned at Bedford and kept in fetters for a year. His gaoler is called Robert de Horepol. There is a Harpole in Northamptonshire, not far from Bedford, and another in Suffolk. Both are spelled with an 'o' in Domesday Book. The fight with 'Ogger' may reflect knowledge that 'Ogier the Breton' held some of Hereward's estates, and still held them in 1086.

An extended and rather romantic story follows in which William de Warenne, Robert Malet and Ivo Taillebois conspire to have Hereward confined in the castle of Rockingham (not Buckingham as in some transcriptions. Domesday records that King William 'ordered a castle to be made there') and Hereward's men, led by Leofric the Deacon and Hogor (his cook!) devise a plan to rescue him and persuade Robert de Horepol to offer only token resistance in the fight that would follow. In return, Hereward insists on releasing de Horepol and his men as Robert, by letting the outlaws know about the Norman plot, had saved his life. He also insists on surrendering himself to the gaoler. Robert de Horepol was apparently so impressed by this that he interceded with King William on Hereward's behalf, convincing him that Hereward was an honourable soldier and no traitor and that he was ready to serve the king faithfully for the rest of his life.

King William, apparently impressed by this rather romantic nonsense, accepted Hereward into his service, returned to him all his family lands and sent writs to the leading men of the district commanding them to return his lands. Hereward thereupon retired from the struggle against the Normans and lived for many years a faithful servant of the king, eventually dying in old age. All of this again is the stuff of legend, reminiscent of the tales told later about other outlaws. That Hereward, whom later writers believed to be son to Leofric, Earl of Mercia, lived on and received back at least some of his family lands, is probably the result of his being confused with the other Hereward, recorded in Domesday Book as still holding lands in Warwickshire and Worcestershire under the Bishop of Worcester and Robert, Count of Mortain. That man had land at Marston Jabbett, Barnacle and Ladbrooke in Warwickshire and at Evenlode and Blockley in Worcestershire, some of which he is said to have held before the Conquest. He is thus the 'man' of the Count of Mortain. No one seriously accepts that this man is the Lincolnshire thegn.

The Crowland Version

It has been argued by some that the tradition at Crowland that Hereward and his wife Turfrida were buried there is reliable, on the grounds that the monks would not have been wrong. It is perhaps more likely that this was an invention intended to attract visitors to the monastery,

just as Glastonbury, in Henry II's reign, was happy to
'discover' the tomb of King Arthur, 'the once and future
king', and that of his wife Guinevere at a time when,
thanks to Geoffrey of Monmouth, all things Arthurian
excited great interest. Glastonbury needed the money
as there had been a disastrous fire. Crowland, which
also made much of its possession of the body of Earl
Waltheof (he was considered to be a martyr by many of
the English), also suffered a damaging fire in 1091.

As for the tale of Hereward's arrest, imprisonment,
release and reconciliation with King William, this is the
stuff of romance. Little of it is supported by any other
source and one is reminded of Robin Hood's reconciliation
with King Richard. It would seem that it is necessary to
look elsewhere for an explanation which might provide
a more likely account of Hereward's fate.

The idea that he was reconciled to the king seems
to stem from the fact that several other leading nobles
were accepted into William's service. Eadric the Wild
submitted in 1070 and proved his usefulness to the king
by serving, presumably with his men, in the campaign
in Scotland. Perhaps that served as a model for those
like Gaimar, who believed that Hereward was accepted
into William's service and went with him to Maine. The
other examples are less happy. Edwin and Morcar were
accepted by William not once but at least twice, though
it did them no good. Edwin reneged, with Morcar, in
1071 and was slain by a band of Normans after betrayal
by three of his own servants (which might again have
provided a model for Gaimar's account) and Morcar,
who submitted after William won his way on to the Isle,
expecting again to be accepted, was imprisoned for life.
Earl Cospatrick submitted, albeit through intermediaries
and at a safe distance, and was briefly recognised again
as Earl of Northumbria, but neither trusted the other and
the Earl took refuge with King Malcolm, becoming Earl

of Dunbar. Earl Waltheof submitted, like Cospatrick, after the great rising in the North, was used by William as a replacement for Cospatrick in Northumbria, became involved in the Rising of the Earls in 1075 and was executed by beheading – the English punishment. As Sir Charles Oman remarked, 'William's enemies had a way of disappearing either into captivity or into the grave.' Why then, should Hereward have trusted him?

But Eadric was the most powerful and influential thegn on the Welsh Marches and all the others were earls, while Hereward was an outlaw who had already lost all his lands. There is no obvious reason why William should have accepted such a man into his service. To give him back his lands would only annoy those Norman barons to whom they had been given. In fact the vast majority of king's thegns had either (a) already submitted and retained at least some of their lands as collaborators with the new regime, or (b) were dead because of involvement in the battles of 1066 or those of the rebellions or (c) had fled into exile in Scotland, Denmark or Flanders. It is notable that the original intention of those who gathered at Ely with Earl Morcar, which after the meeting at Welle included Hereward, was to spend the winter there and then go into exile somewhere overseas, only to be prevented from doing so by King William's blockade. They then decided on resistance, perhaps hoping that the Danes would return.

Another Exile?

Of those who went into exile, little or nothing is known. Some ended up serving in the Varangian Guard of the Byzantine Emperors. Some argue that such was the fate of Siward Barn, who was released in William Rufus' reign from his imprisonment for involvement in the resistance at Ely. He is alleged to be the 'Earl Sigurd' who served at Byzantium. As has been well said, it is thanks to the story of Hereward as told in the *Liber Eliensis* and the *Gesta Herewardi*, and retold by Charles Kingsley in his well-known novel, that Hereward has come to symbolise the English resistance to the Norman Conquest. But, in the light of the contradictions in the sources about his ultimate fate, it seems more than likely that he too was one of the exiles. After all, even the *Gesta* calls him an exile as well as an outlaw, even if the immediate reference is to his exile before the Conquest. There is evidence to support this idea. The first piece is very mysterious; not of itself but in its provenance.

Lt-Gen. Harward, author in 1896 of *Hereward the Saxon Patriot*, maintains that he found in a book variously described as *Historia Ecclesia Eliensis* or as *The Great Book of Ely* (which would seem to be a reference to the *Liber Eliensis* but is not) the following fascinating story. He says that a certain Wilburga of 'Taunton' (i.e. Terrington), Norfolk, made a will when she married a certain 'Hereward' in the reign of Henry II. She left one carucate of land to the church of Lynn with instructions that prayers be said 'for Hereward his father and Hereward the Exile his grandfather'. If this could be verified, it would show descent in the male line of heirs of a man called Hereward who was, like the Hereward of the *Gesta*, an exile.

Although no connection can be established with the Lincolnshire man, there is another curiously similar entry in Abbot Baldwin of Bury's *Feudal Book*, a twelfth-century collection of documents from that abbey recording the lands of the abbey's men in Suffolk. Between 1121 and 1148 Abbot Anselm issued a charter recording the gift to the abbey of 'Goda, daughter of Hereward and all the land of Hereward with her', presumably on the occasion of her presentation as a novice. It was a gift of everything Hereward held wheresoever it was. He and his heirs were to hold the land 'peacefully and quietly and honourably', under the abbot, 'just as the grandfather and father of Hereward and he himself had held it in the vill of (Great) Barton'. There were other Herewards in this document: 'Hereuard' held two acres and received two denarii (pence) in Tostock in Henry I's time and a 'Walter Hereward' (it was common to have a Norman and an English name) witnesses a charter recording a grant by Abbot Hugh from Henry II's reign. In themselves these entries show only that there was a family of Herewards in Suffolk in the twelfth century (though the grandfather would have been born in the eleventh) and perhaps that it was not unknown for families to bestow the name on their children because of its heroic associations. It also strengthens the case for the Wilburga entry being genuine, even if that also only shows the existence of a similar family of Herewards in Norfolk. One oddity is that the subject of the Great Barton entry is called Goda, since this is, according to Pseudo-Ingulf, also the name of the wife of 'Radin' Count of Hereford who was related ('*cognatus*') to Leofric of Bourne, Hereward's alleged father according to this source.

The conclusion to be drawn from the confusion over the exact nature of Hereward's fate, taken together with the known fact that many English thegns became exiles during William I's reign, is that it can be conjectured that Hereward also went into exile, again, after a short sojourn in the Brunneswald as an outlaw. From there he might also have had a small part in the rebellion of the earls, which would explain the confusion in the *Liber Eliensis*. So legends began to gather about his name, especially as no one really knew what had become of him. If he did go into exile, then it was perhaps back to Flanders that he went, where he knew several influential people and where he might have been able to find employment as a mercenary soldier once more. It is also not impossible that, providing he survived, he eventually returned to England, perhaps in the reign of William Rufus when his fame and exploits might well have been forgotten, using money earned abroad to buy himself an estate, maybe in Norfolk or Suffolk, where he eventually died. Perhaps, after all, he did end by arranging his burial at Crowland. But all these can only be put forward as interesting possibilities: there is no evidence for them as yet.

As will be considered subsequently, the late sources for Hereward's ancestry and descendants also provide a family tree tracing Hereward's descents in the female line. This material comes from the fourteenth century and derives ultimately from the pedigree-makers of that century. The claim is that Hereward and Turfrida had a daughter, variously named as Turfrida after her mother or Godiva (after her supposed grandmother?) and that she married a Norman knight in the service of Abbot Turold called Hugh d'Envermeu (the surname is spelt in various incorrect ways in the sources). He in turn is said to have had a daughter who married a minor baron called Richard de Rullos, alleged to be a chamberlain to the king, and that his daughter in turn married Baldwin fitzGilbert. David Roffe, in a recent discussion of the Barony of Bourne and its connection with Hereward, suggests that Turfrida's daughter originally married Ogier the Breton, recorded in Domesday as holding lands previously held by Hereward, and then married Hugh d'Envermeu, which complicates the picture even further. Roffe, however, produces only argument and not solid proof for his suggestions.

Lands formerly belonging to Hereward did end up in the hands of the descendants of Baldwin fitzGilbert, that is, in the Wakes, who were Lords of Bourne, like the de Rullos brothers. Baldwin married the daughter of Richard de Rullos as can be shown from the famous Pipe

Roll, 33 Henry I, but that Richard de Rullos married the daughter of Hugh d'Envermeu and that Hugh married Hereward's daughter depends on the testimony of the *History of Crowland* by the Pseudo-Ingulf, written in around 1370, an account which is contradicted by other known facts. It is also the case that Ogier passed his fief (*feudum*) to a son called Ralph. As Ogier was a Breton, it is possible that his son Ralph is that 'Ralf de Dol' who figures in Gaimar's account of the death of Hereward, which would at least explain where Gaimar obtained the name.

One thing is certain: by the twelfth century, 'Hereward' had become a name to conjure with, to which all sorts of stories and legends became attached, about his ancestry, his descendants and his achievements.

II

Hereward, the Barony of Bourne, and a Family Called Wake

According to the Pipe Roll of 31 Henry I, a member of the powerful Clare Family, Baldwin fitzGilbert, younger son of Gilbert de Clare and so brother of the Earl of Pembroke, rendered account to the Treasury for £301 16s 4d, of which he had paid in £35, for the king's permission to have the land of William de Rullos (Roulours, in Calvados) together with the daughter of his brother Richard, whose name was Adelina, in matrimony. As William was Lord of the Barony of Bourne, Baldwin inherited the barony, or perhaps Henry I created it anew for his benefit. He need not have received it just because he married Adelina because Richard de Rullos was still alive. He is recorded as rendering account for land in Westmoreland. According to the Northamptonshire Survey, which comes from Henry I's reign, four hides were held in Watford 'de feudo Baldwini filii Gilberti' (of the fief of Baldwin fitzGilbert) and at Welleford a certain William de Wyvill held four hides and a 'great' virgate while 'Adam' had one hide and a half in the same place again, de feudo Baldewyni filii Gilberti. This was land belonging to his own fief which was not a barony, though it could have been incorporated in his barony of Bourne after he received it.

Baldwin fitzGilbert was Sheriff of Berkshire in 1126, and in the years that followed his marriage he became a benefactor of Deeping Priory and founder of Bourne Priory in 1138. He was a prominent supporter of King Stephen and delivered the speech to the king's troops before the battle of Lincoln in 1141. His son Roger became a monk and his daughter Emma married a rising minor lord, called Hugh Wac or Wake, son of Geoffrey Wac who died around 1150. In his turn, Hugh Wake became Lord of Bourne, about 1166. He seems to have died in 1172. His son, whose name is recorded in the *Chronicle of Hugh Candidus*, was Baldwin Wake, ancestor of the Wakes of Northamptonshire. A little is known about Geoffrey Wac as he held land in Guernsey, and in Normandy in the Cotentin, and his son Hugh refers to his father's land in Guernsey in a charter of 1168 given to the Abbey of Longues.

As Hugh was at King Stephen's Court at Stamford in 1142, Geoffrey was probably dead by then. There are a few references to Hugh in the records, paying scutage, and making gifts for the souls of his father and mother, for those of Baldwin fitzGilbert and Hugh's own wife, Baldwin's daughter Emma. In his return to the inquest into knights' fees held by Henry II in 1166, the *Cartae Baronum*, he answered for ten and one-eighth fees; one fee from Bourne, his wife's inheritance (with an acknowledgement by Hugh that William de Rullos was his predecessor), and fees held from Humphrey de Bohun, Baldwin fitzGilbert Earl of Gloucester, St Albans Abbey, Simon Earl of Northampton and two from the Bishop of Durham. Some were of the 'old enfeoffment' dating to Henry I's time and others of the 'new enfeoffment' created more recently.

It was from this family of Wake that the cognomen 'the Wake' came to be attached to the name of Hereward because the Wakes claimed descent from him, adopting him as their ancestor. The phrase 'the Wake' is not recorded as attached to Hereward's name until the fourteenth century when he appears in the *Annales Burgo-Spaldenses* (or so-called *Chronicle of Abbot John*) as 'le Wake'. Later, in 1407, evidence of marriage was presented for Edmund de Holland, Earl of Kent, in which, courtesy of the pedigree-makers, he claimed descent in the female line from a daughter of Turfrida. (See Cott. Chart XIII 9 Role de la Généalogie des seigneurs de Brunne et de Deping.) It might be an independent record of the same material as appears in other sources. The genealogy could have been prepared for the benefit of the earl as an attempt to create a noble lineage for him. Hereward is killed after a quarrel with his 'son-in-law' Hugh d'Envermeu, a fate dimly reflected in Gaimar's version of events where he is set upon by a band of Normans (though this more nearly reflects Edwin's fate). It was also claimed that Richard de Rullos, in around 1100, had married a granddaughter of Hereward, called Godiva. Thereafter the line passes to Baldwin fitzGilbert and the Wakes. As Edmund de Holland died in 1408 without issue, his earldom became extinct and the baronies he held, Wake, Woodstock and Holland, fell into abeyance. The present Baronets are descended from a cadet branch of the family.

It has been argued that the Wake genealogy contains genuine traditions because some material in it cannot be accounted for by the suggestion that it was devised for Edmund de Holland's greater glory (Hereward's death; Earl Dolfin's wife) but this may only reflect poor editing. For comparison, one can consider the nineteenth-century genealogy, prepared for an aspiring branch of the Boyd family of Kilmarnock, which traces their ancestry back to Banquo and Fleance, as descended through an unnamed daughter from 'Duff, 78th king of Scotland, son of Malcolm I'. Yet these people were invented by Shakespeare. This document also does not shrink from mentioning the violent deaths of some who figure in that Boyd genealogy, or the murders they committed.

It was during this period, 1350–1450, that 'Ingulf' wrote his *Historia Croylandensis*, in which he claimed that Richard de Rullos married the daughter and heiress of 'Hugh de Evermue', i.e. Envermeu, 'Lord of Bourne and Depyng', and that she was Hereward's granddaughter. Yet he makes Richard a contemporary of Hereward so his chronology in this as in so much else is erroneous. He also claimed that Richard was the king's chamberlain. That would have meant William Rufus, but there is no indication in any of the documents witnessed by Richard and his brother William that either of them was a chamberlain. What is known is that their father was called Ilbert and had been a tenant of Hugh, Earl of Chester. They are quite well documented, witnessing charters and writs of Henry I. Almost the last record of Richard de Rullos is in the Pipe Roll of 1131, where he is said to owe one mark of gold that he may be treated justly in his lord's court.

William had no heir and his lands passed to Richard who, in addition to his daughter, had three sons, Richard, Robert and William, but they did not inherit Bourne because fitzGilbert bought it from the king with the hand of Adelina. There is a charter issued by Richard de Rullos in Henry I's reign addressed to his men, both French and English, granting land to 'Errald' his *'nepos'* in Skeeby in Easby, Yorkshire, to be held of Robert son of Harsculf, his man. It shows that Richard's overlord was Count Alan of Richmond. An inquest into the lands of Wilsford Priory, which had possibly been founded by Hugh d'Envermeu, claims that lands given to the priory by Hugh were held by the prior from Baldwin Wake (son of Hugh Wake) and that Baldwin held them from the king, which emphasises again that the Wake lands had come to them through Baldwin fitzGilbert, who had obtained some of d'Envermeu's lands from Henry I.

Some Light in Dark Corners

As for Richard's daughter Adelina, she had acquired before
1140 half of the fief of the Breton Enisan de Musard,
through her mother who was 'Emma uxor Ricardi de
Rullos'. She was co-heiress with Garsienna, wife of
Roald the Constable of Richmond (North Yorkshire),
to Enisan de Musard in the Honour of Richmond. The
Lords of Richmondshire were Bretons and had brought
many men with them from Brittany. Enisan de Musard
was Baldwin's daughter Emma's grandfather. Garsienna
was the daughter of Enisan's eldest son and the two girls,
Emma (wife of Richard) and Garsienna, were sisters.
This means that Richard de Rullos cannot have married
a daughter of Hugh d'Envermeu. No matter what else
may be said, this alone breaks the connection between
the Wakes and Hereward.

Hugh d'Envermeu was brother not of Abbot Turold,
but of another Turold who was Bishop of Bayeux. Hugh
is witness to six writs and charters and was succeeded,
after death, in his lands at Envermeu by Rayner of
Envermeu, by 1115. According to the Cartulary of St
Laurent d'Envermeu and the *Liber Vitae* of Thorney,
he married a woman called Agnes, said to be heiress
of Bourne. She would in all likelihood have been the
daughter of Ogier the Breton. Hugh, therefore, cannot
be said to have married a daughter of Hereward's wife
Turfrida (as Ingulf claims). That Hugh's land somehow
passed to William de Rullos is shown by Charter No. 1577
(Regesta II) *c.* 1129 at Rouen to St Laurent d'Envermeu,
in which Henry I confirms an earlier charter which had
confirmed its possession of land in England, that is, 'what
Baldwin fitzGilbert had granted to it of the land which
had belonged to Hugh d'Envermeu'. Even if William de
Rullos had married a daughter of Hugh d'Envermeu
(dying without issue) and so inherited land as his wife's

marriage portion, there is no evidence that she was related to Hereward. Nor is there a shred of evidence to suggest that Ogier married either Turfrida or her daughter, as David Roffe has suggested. There is no documentary evidence to support such an idea and there is a further argument against it. According to the *Gesta Herewardi*, supported for what it is worth by Ingulf, Turfrida became a nun at Crowland and was even said to have died and been buried there. Many wives and daughters of English thegns, wishing to avoid being required or forced to marry a Norman against their will, sought refuge in convents. Archbishop Lanfranc, when asked to rule on the question whether a woman who had done this and subsequently was found to have no real vocation could be released from her vows, states categorically that many women had sought refuge to avoid being forced to marry. It does look as though Turfrida, after her repudiation by Hereward, did exactly what others were doing, which makes it unlikely that she contracted a second marriage. No, it is land that connects these men. The reign of Henry I was a time of great territorial changes, as land changed hands and fiefs and baronies were built up out of the estates of many smaller landowners.

Hugh Candidus, writing about the lands of Hugh 'de Euremu' as he has it, states that Baldwin Wake held land in Deeping, Plumtree and Stowe as a fee for three knights and also the fee of one knight 'in Witham and Barholm of the land of Asfort'. He is said to hold them by rendering service to the Abbot of Peterborough. These were all lands that Abbot Turold alienated and they are held of the Church, so that they did not come to the barony through any marriage. 'Asfort' or Asfrothr was one of Abbot Turold's men and these estates are shown as held by him in Domesday Book. Some of this land had been held by Hereward, and Asfrothr was one of his successors, at Witham-on-the-Hill, Manthorpe, Toft and

Lound and at Barholme and Stowe (see the *Descriptio Terrarum* of the abbey dated to 1071–86). The other main recipient of land previously belonging to Hereward was Ogier the Breton, who also received Morcar's estate at Bourne. According to the '*Descriptio Militum de Abbatia de Burgo*', a list of the abbey's lands dated to 1100–20, 'Hugh de Euremou' held two hides and eight bovates in demesne in Lincolnshire and did service to the abbey for two knights' fees.

Out of various pieces of land, in Lincolnshire, Leicestershire, Hertfordshire and Northamptonshire, Henry I created a barony for William de Rullos, with its 'caput' or chief seat at Bourne. It is known that Bourne itself was already the name of an established fief because, in the Northamptonshire Survey, Ralph the son of Ogier held two hides and one virgate in Thrapstone 'of the fief of Bourne'. There is no record of any of the alleged marriages to daughters or granddaughters of Hereward. It would seem that the fourteenth-century writers, and those who followed them, assumed that the lands had passed from one man to the other through marriage, and that, as at least some of the lands had once belonged to Hereward, they had been acquired as the dowry of his daughter, which was a very common way for land to be passed on where there was no male heir. Of 187 baronies from the Norman period studied by Sanders (*English Baronies*), thirty-two descended in the female line. Examples of those who married English heiresses include Ivo Taillebois (Lucy 'the Countess', daughter of Thorold of Lincoln), Colsuen, Alfred of Lincoln, Colegrim, Robert Malet and Durand Malet. Men in the twelfth century would have assumed that this was the case at Bourne.

These lands came by the gift of Henry I. Richard de Rullos, for example, held just under eight carucates in Thorpe and Twyford, which in 1086 had been held by the king. When the king restored land to Peterborough Abbey in 1114, 'as when Turold was alive and dead' (Regesta II No. 1038), and also that which had been 'usurped by evil men in the early part of the king's reign', Asfrothr, or Asfort, who held Hereward's manor of Witham-on-the-Hill, is named as one of Turold's knights whose land was now restored. Baldwin fitzGilbert witnesses the charter along with Bishop Hervey of Ely.

The Bourne barony included the 'soke' of Bourne and other sokelands and estates in Rippingale and Laughton in Lincolnshire, Kilby, Leicestershire, and 'Austhorpe', Rutland, which went to Ogier's son Ralph in around 1105 and eventually to fitzGilbert by the 1120s or 1130s. All was probably held by Baldwin in right of his wife Adelina and as a result of his payment to the king. From that inheritance there also came lands listed in Domesday for Geoffrey de Cambrai in Lincolnshire, Leicestershire and Rutland and the fief of Baldwin the Fleming also in Lincolnshire. The Lords of Bourne, as successors to Geoffrey, seized Witham-on-the-Hill.

The links in the chain that leads from Baldwin fitzGilbert back through the de Rullos brothers and Hugh d'Envermeu and so to Ogier the Breton are fragile to say the least and, as explained above, the marriage of a daughter of Ogier called Agnes to Hugh d'Envermeu breaks the chain completely (Hereward cannot have had a daughter or a granddaughter called Agnes; a French name would never have been given, as early as that, to the daughter of an Anglo-Danish family), yet an explanation for the claim that these lands came from Hereward, and by marriage, is needed. The real reason, which may have carried little weight in the twelfth century, lies in Hereward's status as the son and heir of a great king's thegn who was the predecessor in Lincolnshire of those who held these estates in 1086, especially Ogier the Breton who held Bourne as a fief. Lawsuits did proceed based on the evidence of Domesday Book, but in practice the de facto tenures recorded in 1086 meant that little action was taken to restore lands to their 'rightful' owners, especially perhaps after William I's death. Possession was nine points of the law.

In the twelfth century, however, hereditary right had become a more potent argument and was seen as a more plausible explanation for Baldwin's claim. Ingulf in the fourteenth century did not have access to the full facts and knew only what had been claimed. Ogier and his son had naturally had an interest in the fief, and opinion would have demanded that a daughter of Hereward had married one or the other, whether this had happened or not. So what we have in Ingulf and in the genealogy provided a not unreasonable explanation for the origins of the Bourne barony. In due course, Baldwin's daughter married Hugh Wake and the family continued from there, although they are only styled Wakes of Bourne after 1241.

Hugh or Hugo Wac, who died around 1176, father of Baldwin Wake (died 1201) was a man of Humphrey IV de Bohun and the number of his knights' fees appears in that baron's 'Carta', the return to Henry II's inquiry into his barons' holdings in 1166. Richard de Rullos married Emma, heiress of the Breton Enisan de Musard. Therefore, his wife was Breton and she was not the daughter of Hugh d'Envermeu as the *Historia Croylandensis* claims. This also seems to break any link between the de Rullos brothers and Ogier the Breton, and even more certainly breaks any tenuous putative link with Hereward.

Hereward in Fact and Fiction

What most people know about Hereward is derived from a hazy recollection of stories drawn from Charles Kingsley's novel of 1867, *Hereward the Wake*, or from the comments of historians and writers who briefly round off their accounts of the opening stage of the Norman Conquest with a summary of the rebellions against King William between 1067 and 1072, and mention the capture of Ely as an afterthought.

In fact there is a considerable amount of information not only about the various rebellions and King William's response to them but also about Hereward himself. This can be gleaned from the writings of medieval chroniclers, the pages of Domesday Book, and very many other sources of information such as royal writs and charters. Despite this, most major histories of the period and even the biographical studies of King William say little about the rebellions and even less about Hereward, unless it is to dismiss his exploits as some kind of sideshow.

However, in more recent years scholars have investigated various aspects of the Hereward saga. Cyril Hart has explored the Fenland background and looked at the identity of some of Hereward's men, the Companions. David Roffe has looked at the creation of the barony of Bourne and considered whether there is any truth in the

claims of the Wakes to have inherited their lands from
Hereward as a result of a series of marriages involving
his alleged descendants, none of which can really be
substantiated and which are indeed contradicted by other
evidence. This claim was originally dismissed as unproven
by the Victorian scholar and genealogist J. H. Round, who
did so much to explode some of the genealogical claims
made by those who derived their alleged descent from
Norman times. Round and his great rival E. A. Freeman
saw the inconsistencies in the Hereward material. Round
recognised that there might be some truth behind the
adventures in Flanders, and Freeman saw Hereward as
a champion of English liberty. H. W. C. Davis in 1905
saw the whole Hereward cycle as the product of ballad-
mongers and regarded most of it as fiction, except for
that part which is also related in the *Liber Eliensis*. He
regarded it as natural to assume that an Ely writer would
be well informed about William's assault on the Isle. Like
others he notes that Hereward was seen as the champion
of 'the English national cause'. It sometimes is the case
that where evidence is lacking, historians can only make
conjectures based on outward appearances, or perhaps
from their own, often subconscious, prejudices.

Elisabeth van Houts has investigated the continental
background to Hereward's exploits in Scaldemariland
and shown that they are not easily dismissed as pure
fiction. Others have looked at the surviving material
about Hereward from other angles, considering that the
impact of an understanding of his place in history depends
on recognising what sort of literature has survived and
considering the motives of the writers who produced
it. Not all of them were writing or intending to write
straightforward history.

There are some more eccentric views also, from writers
with their own axe to grind, such Lt-Gen. Harward,
author in 1896 of *Hereward the Saxon Patriot*. This

work not only attempts to show, albeit unsuccessfully for the most part, that anyone with a name remotely resembling that of Hereward, such as Harwood, Harward or Harvard, is probably his descendant, but also traces his ancestry back through a succession of non-existent earls to AD 600.

Some historians, too, allow the prejudices or preconceptions of their own times to affect their judgement. E. A. Freeman in his mammoth study of the Norman Conquest presents Hereward as representative of patriotic, almost democratic, eleventh-century Englishmen very like the Victorian parliamentarians with whom he was familiar. Douglas Jerrold in 1944 saw Hereward as an archetypal quisling, ready to betray England to the Danes, yet a quisling is a collaborator who helps the invader take over the government of the country and is a term more rightly used of those like Archbishop Ealdred and Regenbald 'the Chancellor'. They and others were only too ready to explain the workings of English government to William the Norman and to assist in the transfer of power.

The medieval stories about Hereward fall into three main traditions, emanating from the Fenland monasteries of Peterborough, Ely and Crowland. Each of these had a different tale to tell and differing priorities which affect the way in which Hereward is depicted.

Then there are the novelists in the nineteenth and twentieth centuries. Hereward is the leading figure in Kingsley's work. He was climbing aboard a bandwagon set rolling in 1834 by Bulwer Lytton with his *Last Days of Pompeii* and *Harold, Last of the Saxons*, 1848, when it became fashionable to write 'last of the line' novels. It has been suggested also that it was part of a great Victorian love affair with the Danelaw. There was a great burst of writing about Anglo-Saxons, about the Sagas and stories of Norsemen. Beowulf was published and in

1884, in a bid to reclaim the Fens culturally, the Revd
G. S. Streatfield wrote *Lincolnshire and the Danes*. To
this can be added Lt-Gen. Harward's strange effusion,
Hereward the Saxon Patriot, 1896.

One view of 'Hereward the Wake' is to see it as a
romance or saga, the narrative dressed in saga motifs,
with much genealogical matter, the introduction of
the supernatural (Hereward is given magic armour by
Turfrida). There are berserkers and elderly Vikings, even
the Geste of Robin Hood is used (in the tale of Hereward
in disguise). Kingsley perhaps intended to give a regional
identity to England such as Sir Walter Scott's writings
had given to Scotland.

Charles Kingsley, who was not only a novelist but
Regius Professor of History at Cambridge, provides the
bridge between the historians and the novelists. *Hereward
the Wake* has an historical prologue in which Kingsley
defends his thesis that Hereward was son to Earl Leofric
of Mercia. There is much useful historical matter amidst
the usual Victorian views, such as the argument that King
Edward was pro-Norman, and prejudiced comment
about medieval clergy, yet much of what he says is
marred by a tendency to accept evidence uncritically, as
when he suggests that the fifteenth-century genealogy of
Hereward was 'no doubt taken from previously existing
records or the old tradition of the family'. He does
seem to be the first to emphasise that the circle from
which Hereward came was Anglo-Danish, but does not
follow this through. While accepting that Abbot Brand
was Hereward's uncle, he fails to see the contradiction
between that fact and his own assertion that Hereward
was the son of Earl Leofric.

The novel itself follows the outline of Hereward's story
as given in the *Gesta Herewardi*, including the adventures
in Cornwall, where he invents 'Alef', a Cornish 'kinglet'.
He anticipates later findings in identifying Scaldemariland

with the 'meres of the Scheldt' but persists in accepting Bourne not only as Hereward's estate but as the main residence of Earl Leofric and occupied in the novel by Countess Godiva. Finally, Kingsley departs from the *Gesta* account and has Hereward slain in a Norman trap, in a version of his final end derived from Geoffrey Gaimar, but still has him laid to rest at Crowland. He is termed 'the last of the English'.

From then on a number of others have written their versions of the story, but none are even remotely near the historical Hereward, and Kingsley's work remains more acceptable than the others. One interesting point is that only Kingsley inserts the story from the *Peterborough Chronicle* and Hugh Candidus about the attack on Peterborough. Some other novels, covering the period from the 1890s to more recent times, can be surveyed as typical: 1897 edition of *The Camp of Refuge* by C. MacFarlane (first published in 1844 and again between 1846 and 1848 and so preceding Kingsley); *For Hereward and Freedom*, A. Edwards Chapman, 1933; *The Last Englishman*, H. Weenolson, 1952; *The First Englishman*, Russell Thorndike (no date but possibly earlier than Weenolson).

Each can be briefly considered. MacFarlane's work parts company with historical fact almost immediately and the editor of the 1897 edition, G. L. Gomme, provides an introduction stressing his difference from Kingsley. He also points to Bulwer Lytton's influence. MacFarlane discounts the whole of the 'Leofric the Deacon' material in the *Gesta Herewardi*, seeing this as part of the cycle of myths which gathered round the name. He prefers to have Hereward learning his trade as a soldier in Wales, and taking part in the battles of Stamford Bridge and Hastings. Gomme stresses the idea that Hereward was called 'the Exile' in his own time and briefly relates the adventures attributed to Hereward by 'Leofric' and the story of the Norman attack on Ely with Hereward's part in it.

In the novel itself the story begins in 1070 and characters, monks at Spalding, discuss the activities of Ivo Taillebois. The correct historical background is described and thereafter the tale is mainly told through the actions of Elfric, a novice at Spalding. Hereward is said to be in exile in Flanders, intending to settle there. However he is called back to England by Abbot Thurstan and brings much-needed weaponry and men. He is accompanied by the entirely fictitious Girolamo of Salerno, an expert in the use of fire and catapults.

Most of the novel then follows, though with little exactitude, the traditional course of events at Peterborough and Ely. One interesting difference is that Hereward believes King Harold escaped after Hastings and expects his return. In his version also, Alftruda plays a more prominent role and it is she who bears Hereward's (unnamed) heir, a boy child. King William is said to build bridges as well as a causeway in the Fens and his men cross smaller streams by means of portable bridges.

A. Edwards Chapman's *For Hereward and Freedom* centres on the adventures of Edgar, son of a charcoal burner, who assists the English rebels, beginning the story in 1071 after Hereward has established himself at Ely. The whole tale is really about Edgar, and Hereward is relatively a necessary background figure. The story touches on real events, such as the struggle against King William and the building and destruction of causeways at Aldreth, but the end of that causeway is said to be only a quarter of a mile from Ely. There is a fictitious dramatic ending with Hereward fighting an unknown Norman knight who beats him to his knees and forces him to surrender. The knight removes his helm and reveals that he is King William himself. Hereward is reconciled to the king and becomes his man. Happy ending!

Russell Thorndike's *The First Englishman* is equally unhistorical. He begins his story at Rouen in 1069 where Ivo Taillebois, 'the king's supreme commander', had come to escort a 'Princess' (later named 'Arletine') to England. Hereward is presented as 'Earl of Mercia and Lord of Bourne' and calls himself 'the Wake'. He also has a castle at Bourne. Most of the tale is one of conflict between Hereward and Ivo. Hereward 'marries' a Spanish-looking girl called Terecha. Ely already has a 'mighty cathedral'. Interestingly the attackers at Ely use a pontoon bridge, which Hereward duly sinks by holing with arrows the bladders of air supporting it. King William calls himself 'Bill the Bastard' and talks about 'our Great Survey of Domesday'. Hereward marries Arletine, having left Terecha in Rouen with his child. His marriage to her is said to be invalid because it was not performed by a priest. By his marriage to Arletine, Hereward makes an enemy in Ascelin, who seeks to trap and kill him near Ely. The trap is sprung, Hereward fights heroically against tremendous odds, as in Geoffrey Gaimar, and is mortally wounded. Martin Lightfoot gets his wounded lord into the abbey where all is in ruins and the monks dead or dying, having been overwhelmed by Ivo Taillebois. The dying Hereward fires the library and staircase, which engulfs Ivo, who has been stabbed by Martin Lightfoot. Hereward is last seen, like King Arthur, being taken away in a barge accompanied by three women, Lady Godiva, Terecha and her daughter. All good fun, but not history.

The last of these works is H. Weenolson's book, *The Last Englishman*. In a postscript the author does admit to taking liberties with chronology and that the work is fictional. She begins her tale with the comet of 1066 and moves rapidly to the return of Hereward from Jerusalem, Sicily and Constantinople. He takes refuge in the 'Gronneswald', where he rescues, and falls for, a lady called here Althya. Hereward, called Leofricsson, has been disinherited by King William whom he sees as a usurper and a robber. Encountering supporters of Waltheof, who is the king's prisoner, he is enlisted in planning a rebellion during which Waltheof will be released. There is a scene set in the White Tower (which in fact would not yet have existed) between the king and his family. Hereward sends a thegn called Letwold to enter the tower in the assumed guise of a harper, in order to contact Waltheof.

Hereward's main opponent is called Guy de Lussac, who tells the king about the death of 'Oger of Bayeux' (not the Breton) and Hereward's attack on 'Bourne castle'. Waltheof escapes from the tower and he and Hereward lead the rebels, helped by Eadric the Wild, and capture York. Hereward then allies himself with a Dane, 'Asbiorn', who demands money before he will assist the English.

The scene shifts to Cambridgeshire and Belsar's Hill. Hereward has taken refuge at Ely and William has found that it is too hazardous to use his fleet and attack by water. Hereward is still supported by Waltheof and Eadric and there is no sign of Morcar. Hereward spies on the king's army, the potter story, and William builds his causeway. In this story the witch or pythoness is Guy de Lussac's idea. There is, as in other versions, the firing of the reeds and the causeway, but William realises that this trick cannot be performed a second time and renews his assault.

Guy de Lussac captures Edgytha (Hereward's mother) in order to lure Hereward to him at his manor of 'Cruc Maur'. Meanwhile, Hereward and Eadric the Wild sack Torksey. After that Hereward and Eadric are ambushed at a ford, Eadric is shot by Guy and William fitzOsbern captures Hereward. He is taken to the king at Lincoln, and he offers Hereward an earldom if he will submit.

Hereward refuses, spitting in the king's face, and is handed over to Guy. There is a fight and in the end Hereward is stabbed by Guy.

So much for the various ways in which Hereward's story has been told. As can be seen, only Kingsley gets anywhere near the historical facts and even his version is marred by preconceptions about his hero. There are other writers who give what they claim is a more factual account of Hereward. They are no historians, but neither are they novelists. Two examples are given here, linked by a common interest in genealogy. First is a curious work published in 1896 by a Lt-Gen. Thomas Netherton Harward, called *Hereward the Saxon Patriot*.

He begins by rehearsing the usual story of Hereward's descent from noble ancestors but insists on confounding Hereward the Outlaw with the Midland man with land at Marston Jabbett. He claims that Hereward is the younger son of Earl Leofric and that it was he who 'retired to the Isle of Ely after the Conqueror's invasion, to be the general of their forces'. Leofric is variously claimed to have been Earl of Lincoln, then of Chester, of Hereford and finally of Mercia. No evidence is offered for these extraordinary claims. Hereward is not actually outlawed, he says, but 'expatriated', sent out of the country. But as he calls Aelfgar's outlawry an expatriation also, there does not seem to be much difference. He doubts whether Hereward really served Count Baldwin but suggests that Flemish records may cast light on this in the future. The rest of what he says directly about Hereward leans heavily on Geoffrey Gaimar and Pseudo-Ingulf together with the other usual sources.

He insists on attributing various estates in the Midlands to Hereward, such as Coleshill in Warwickshire, and says he held Terrington in Norfolk under Roger Bigod. Domesday Book does not support this claim not that to Coleshill. In the end he has Hereward reconciled to the king, married to Aelfthryth (Alftruda), and at war in Maine where he commanded the English contingent, after which he retires to quiet domestic bliss. Harward dismissed the tragic end described by Gaimar as so much of a stain on William's character that he cannot bring himself to credit it. He prefers the *Gesta Herewardi*'s version. Quite rightly he criticises Gaimar's account as too much in the style of a chorus in a Greek play to be accepted as fact.

Basing his claim on an entry in a volume variously described as *Liber Ecclesiae Eliensis*, the *Great Book of Ely* or *Historia Ecclesiae Eliensis*, he tells a story of a woman called Wilburga living at Terrington, Norfolk, who leaves money to the church of Lynn so that prayers may be said for her husband, Hereward, for Hereward his father and for Hereward the Banished or the Exile, his grandfather. From this he claims that just about every Hereward recorded in medieval documents is descended from these people and so from Hereward himself. Unfortunately all efforts so far to identify this source have failed. It is certainly not the *Liber Eliensis*, of which the first two books are also called 'Historia Ecclesia Eliensis'.

He claims to have used Domesday Book, *Herald's Visitations*, various (unidentified) Harleian manuscripts, other charters and deeds, General and County Histories, Palgrave's *Saxon Commonwealth*, local authorities on heraldry in Worcestershire, Warwickshire and Norfolk, monastic records and a pedigree for Hereward drawn up by St T. Philips FSA for the Revd J. Harward of Hartlebury.

The result of all this is the astonishing claim that the genealogy of Hereward and the Harwards begins in Surrey in AD 600. He then traces the line down through a succession of Earls to Earl Leofric and so to Aelfgar and Hereward his brother. He again quotes the Wilburga

story, now set in reign of Henry II rather than as earlier
under Henry I, and jumps from there to a seventeenth-
century *Herald's Visitations* in Warwickshire. For this he
also cites the church registers of Aldborough St Mary's
and Terrington St Clement's for information about later
Herewards.

At this point he dismisses the name Wake as applied
to Hereward and calls the Wakes doubtful claimants
to belong to Hereward's lineage. He attacks Charles
Kingsley for writing 'as much unintelligible nonsense as
any author of his day' and baldly calls his facts fictions.
Correctly, he points out that the name Wake was not
used before the fifteenth century. He ventures to claim
that coats of arms were in use in the eleventh century and
that Hereward adopted that of Frederick 'de Warenne'
as he was entitled to do because he had killed him. The
family arms of Leofric are then claimed to be a German
Eagle on a bend Gules. Wilburga's story is now put as
occurring in Edward I's reign. After that the book goes
off into a discussion of the various Herewards of the
fourteenth and fifteenth centuries.

Without really producing verifiable evidence,
he produces a family tree for Hereward through
Wilburga's husband to John Hereward of Pebworth or
Bedworth, from whom he claims all Warwickshire and
Worcestershire Herewards and Harwards descend, and
Theobald de Hereward of Aldborough, who is ancestor of
the Herewards of Norfolk. From there he easily connects
all known Herewards, Herwards, Harwards and even
Harvards as members of this widespread clan; and, of
course, includes himself.

It is difficult to know what to make of such a work,
lacking, as it does, all comprehension of what constitutes
historical or genealogical proof. The sole nugget of what
looks like useful fact in it is the story about Wilburga
and that cannot be substantiated, although it does

resemble the similar account in Abbot Baldwin's *Feudal Book* about Goda, wife of Hereward and his father and grandfather, assumed also to be called Hereward, though this is not stated.

The next work is *Hereward* by Victor Head. He certainly distinguishes the fabulous from those events which may have a basis in fact, but writes too early to be aware of the Flanders dimension. He tends to accept the view of H. W. C. David about Hereward's fate, that Crowland would surely not have been entirely wrong. Like so many others, he sees more truth in the Pseudo-Ingulf's account than can easily be accepted. The main problem is that he takes on board rather a lot of Lt Gen. Harward's views. He suggests, citing the reference to it in Davis (*England under the Normans and Angevins*), that the *Liber Eliensis*, dated by Davis to 1174–89, is Harward's *Ely Book*. As has been remarked, the Wilburga story is not in this work and that writer cannot have checked for it. One good thing is that he points out the resemblance between the account of Hereward's (alleged) return to Bourne and the return to Ithaca by Ulysses. Then, in order to fill out his book, he expends a great deal of energy considering matters genealogical, like Lt-Gen. Harward, which has little bearing on the book's main subject, the man Hereward himself.

He does, of course, recite the traditional story, following the *Gesta Herewardi* (in T. Bevis' translation) and takes from Domesday 'the day he fled' to mean 1071. He makes good use of Orderic Vitalis and the *Peterborough Chronicle*, but the book does peter out rather into the above-mentioned genealogical matters.

More interesting are two articles which look at the matter which might have motivated the authors of the *Gesta Herewardi* and other sources of information about Hereward. John Hayward in *Hereward the Outlaw* (J. M. H. Vol. 14 No. 4, 1988) seeks to establish what these sources contribute to an understanding of post-Conquest English consciousness and identity, and Hugh M. Thomas, *The* Gesta Herewardi, *the English and their Conquerors* (A. N. S. xxi 1998), seeks to investigate what were the concerns and interests of the author.

Hayward attributes the *Gesta Herewardi* to Richard of Ely and reviews all the evidence from that work and the other usual sources. He notes that general histories dismiss the matter of Ely 'in a single line based on the hypothesis that Hastings was William's decisive battle', although contemporaries might not have seen it like that. He sees Hereward not as a major political figure, as he certainly wasn't, but correctly as a military leader of ability. He rejects the idea that the intention of those at Ely had been to drive the Normans out of England and suggests that Hereward's idea was to make a nuisance of himself and so compel William to offer him acceptable terms for his submission. His general conclusion is that Hereward was an able guerilla leader and his exploits derive from some genuine traditions. The most important point was that he was English and became an emblem of resistance to a foreign oppressor. Much of the material of his legend found its way into the myth of Robin Hood. His story was written at a time when there was a need for English popular heroes.

Hugh Thomas acknowledges that the *Gesta Herewardi* is the fullest account there is of 'an important leader of the English resistance', despite the many fantastic elements which clutter up the story. He too accepts Richard of Ely as the author and says he is writing 'pseudo-history' to rebut charges of English inferiority in warfare, men who are ignorant of the laws and usages of war. So Hereward becomes a figure of romance and chivalry and represents English success as warriors. The Ely campaign is a series of military disasters for the Normans. So it presents 'the deeds of the magnificent Hereward of the English people',

who fights with sword and lance and is knighted. He is of
noble ancestry and his companions are noble likewise.

As this brief sketch of the various ways in which the
Hereward story has been presented, in both fact and
fiction, by novelists, historians and others, shows, there
are many ways of viewing the man, his history and his
myth. This is by no means a comprehensive review, only
an attempt to give the reader some idea of the wealth
of writing that exists on this theme. Those who wish
to know more will find many useful works listed in the
bibliography.

The last step is to consider the three main medieval
traditions about Hereward. Each comes from a different
monastery and reflects the motives and concerns of the
writers. These three monasteries are Peterborough, Ely
and Crowland.

The Peterborough tradition is found firstly in the
additions from local sources made to the text of the
Peterborough Chronicle. This is found in the Bodleian
Library MS Laud. Misc. 636 and is termed the 'E' text
by editors. It is a manuscript of the twelfth century,
most probably written out at Peterborough by a copyist
using the text of a version of the chronicle compiled
at St Augustine's, Canterbury, at least up to 1061 and
probably to 1121. Only after that latter date does the
text reflect affairs at Peterborough, ending in 1155. The
reason for this is simple. A fire in 1116 destroyed much of
Peterborough and so it is thought a copy of the chronicle
was borrowed from St Augustine's to replace the abbey's
own copy. As he did his work, the scribe added various
items to the text, such as spurious charters, notices of
local events and, of course, the attack on Peterborough by
Hereward and the Danes. It is certainly an interpolation
into the original from which he was copying but is surely
based on local knowledge and not, as has been alleged,
merely invented. The story is found, with additional

detail and information, in the *Peterborough Chronicle of Hugh Candidus* (B. Mus. Add. MS. 39758). Hugh flourished from 1100 to about 1175, and his work is thus mid-twelfth century.

Both sources agree that the attack on Peterborough came before that on Ely, that Hereward was an outlaw and Candidus adds that he was a 'man' of the monks, that is, a tenant holding land from the abbey.

The tradition at Ely is found in the *Liber Eliensis*, from which this book has derived only the account of King William's dealings with Hereward and his capture of the abbey and the town, and in the *Gesta Herewardi*. Much of the text of the *Liber Eliensis* is found also in the work of Master Geoffrey Gaimar, *L'Estorie des Engles*. These three works reflect the Fenland tradition and have in common the fact that the attack on Peterborough took place after that on Ely. Most historians accept that the Peterborough tradition is more likely to be right. Gaimar differs from the other sources in his account of Hereward's end, assassinated by a band of Normans, whereas the *Gesta Herewardi* says (as does the third tradition) that he died at peace with the king. It is difficult to accept Gaimar's account as he is unsupported by any other writer. He might well have been giving his hero a hero's death and could have borrowed the detail from a poem relating the death of Earl Edwin (as the language used by Orderic Vitalis suggests), who was also assassinated by a group of Normans, after betrayal by his own men, and beheaded. Gaimar wrote for Constance, wife of Ralph fitzGilbert, in about 1140 and used various known sources including 'the book of Washingborough' which is thought to have been a now missing version of the *Anglo-Saxon Chronicle*.

Lastly, there is the Crowland tradition as recorded in the *Historia Croylandensis* which purports to be the work of Abbot Ingulf at the end of the eleventh century but which has been shown to be a compilation of the late fourteenth. Despite its late date, 'Ingulf' does contain genuine information. Some of its sources have been identified. Its author was not well educated and makes frequent errors of fact and chronology. He was also a very poor copyist and did not always understand his sources. He knew a variant text of the *Gesta Herewardi* (or copies it very badly) but he gives a number of statements about Hereward which cannot be substantiated and appear to be contradicted by known facts. Nonetheless, it may be that more of his work is true than can be verified. For instance, he seems to be right that some of Hereward's lands passed to Hugh d'Envermeu, a knight in the service of Turold of Peterborough, and that they became the property of Richard de Rullos. But he attributes the transmission to a series of marriages to Hereward's daughter and granddaughter, for which there is no proof. He briefly mentions the resistance of Ely under Edwin and Morcar (though confusing it, as does the *Liber Eliensis*, with the Revolt of the Earls) and knows of Hereward's attack on Peterborough which he too seems to imply took place after the attack on Ely. But his sense of chronology is confused, and the order in which he gives events even more so. Those who wish to rehabilitate this author argue that he could have used material from Orderic Vitalis preserved at Crowland. Orderic wrote a *Vita* of St Guthlac for Prior Wulfwine around 1115 and could have left other writings at Crowland which were then seen by 'Ingulf', but there is no real evidence of this. Orderic himself focussed his attention on the Earls Edwin and Morcar and never mentions Hereward. Other materials certainly might have survived the fire of 1091, rescued perhaps by the real Ingulf as tradition claims. Of this, some poor copies might have survived and been used. The Pseudo-Ingulf did have access to sources, even some sort of records relating to the Domesday Survey and materials written in Old English, but he does not seem to have always translated or understood his materials. His evidence has to be treated with circumspection and accepted only when it can either be confirmed from existing documents or where it fits other known facts.

There are notices of Hereward in the major chronicles, from Florence of Worcester onwards, but these are derived from the earlier accounts and contribute little new information. Hereward is last noticed in the *Annales Burgo-Spaldenses*, previously known erroneously as the *Chronicle of Abbot John*. This is also late fourteenth or perhaps early fifteenth century and consists, as the name now used suggests, of a series of annals recording events to distinguish one year from another. Taken together, they tell of Hereward's return from exile and his taking of revenge for the loss of his lands, his conflict with King William and with Abbot Turold. It is the first text to call Hereward 'Le Wake'. It correctly records Abbot Brand's death in 1069 and calls him Hereward's paternal uncle. The castle mound at Peterborough, 'Mount Turold', is said to be Abbot Turold's work and he is said to have given sixty-two hides of abbey lands to his hired knights for protecting him against Hereward. The latter is credited with capturing the abbot and securing a ransom of 30,000 silver marks (which if a ransom were true, would be 30 or 300 marks, not this vast sum). Turold dies in 1098. Such facts in this as can be checked, as for instance in the *Gesta Herewardi* or Hugh Candidus, seem verifiable.

Appendices

Appendix 1: Hereward's Companions

Hereward's associates before, during and after the defence of Ely fall into a number of separate categories. There are those associated with him in 'outlawry' and certainly in opposition to Norman rule, and there are those who joined him at Ely who form two separate classes; the former leaders of the opposition to King William in the Midlands and the North and the leading men of the East Midlands and East Anglia who had either already seen their lands confiscated, possibly for previous opposition, or who feared that it would not be long before they too lost lands and office. Each group is listed and considered separately.

The Nobility: Earls, Bishops and Leading Thegns

Earls Edwin and Morcar
These are the sons of Aelfgar, Earl of Mercia and son of the great Earl Leofric. Earl Edwin had succeeded his father Aelfgar by 1063 (the exact date of Aelfgar's death and how he died is unknown) as Earl of Mercia and with his brother Morcar fought and lost the battle of Fulford Gate against Harald Hardrada in 1066. Morcar became

Earl of Northumbria after the expulsion of Earl Tostig
Godwinson by the Northumbrians and he was chosen by
the Northumbrians. The earls fought neither at Stamford
Bridge nor Hastings, presumably because of the heavy
losses they had sustained at Fulford and the consequent
damage to their military reputation.

After the battle they eventually submitted to King
William, and Edwin, at least, received vague promises of
a secure role in the new state and a marriage to a daughter
of the Conqueror which did not materialise. They rebelled
in 1068 but their opposition collapsed at the first sign of
the Conqueror's response and they were in theory received
back into his favour. After the great rising of 1069–70, in
which they played no overt part, they feared imprisonment
by William and fled from his court, wandering in fields
and woods for some six months, before meeting other
rebels, including Hereward, at Welle in Norfolk and took
refuge at Ely, intending, it was said, to go into exile.

William's blockade certainly trapped Morcar and might
have prevented Edwin's departure. The sources contradict
themselves about whether he stayed a long time at Ely
or went north immediately, heading for Scotland, and
about when exactly he left. The Ely tradition believed he
stayed and hints that the earls played a greater part in the
resistance than is apparent in either the *Liber Eliensis* or
the *Gesta Herewardi*.

Earl Edwin did at some time go north, but was betrayed
by three of his own servants and murdered by a group
of Normans who trapped him beside fast-flowing water
where he was cut off by the tide. His betrayers cut off his
head and took it to the king, who executed them. Morcar
continued as titular head of the defenders at Ely, though
accepting Hereward with his greater military experience
as the commander in the field, until towards the end. He
then foolishly accepted assurances of safe conduct and
reconciliation conveyed to him by agents of the king

and surrendered, either just before or during the king's final assault. He was imprisoned for life and, although released by William when the king was on his deathbed, was re-arrested and died in imprisonment.

Bishop Aethelwine of Durham

He was brother, possibly younger, to Aethelric, Bishop of Durham before him. Both seem to have been involved in the northern rising in some way, though the sources are vague as to circumstances. Aethelric had retired in favour of his brother; he found life hard and violent and the people of the north often damaged the interests of the Church, and he took refuge at Peterborough. While there he is said to have excommunicated the outlaws who raided the abbey because they stole some of his own property. King William, for reasons that remain unclear, arrested him and sent him into custody at Westminster. There he died in 1072. His brother Aethelwine promptly fled to Scotland (there were accusations, not necessarily true, that he took money from Durham), and he might have been more involved in the revolt than appears. He had warned Robert de Commines, who had billeted himself in the Bishop's House, to expect trouble, but had been ignored. De Commines and his men were attacked by the Northumbrians and slaughtered. Perhaps Aethelwine feared William's wrath. His first idea had been to go into exile, perhaps at Cologne, but storms frustrated that idea and he ended up in Scotland. From there he joined the thegn Siward Barn and sailed down the east coast, meeting Earl Morcar near Ely. He then took refuge on the Isle and after the defeat was arrested, imprisoned at Abingdon and died shortly afterwards.

Siward Barn

He was a wealthy and powerful thegn with 'sake and soke' (an indication that he was a king's thegn) in Derbyshire,

Nottinghamshire and Lincolnshire, and lands totalling over 100 hides and sixty carucates in seven shires. He was reported as in the company of Edgar the Aetheling at Wearmouth after the failure of the northern rebellion, and the harrying of the North, and to have accompanied him to Scotland. He had probably already lost all his lands (which went to Henry de Ferrers) and had nothing left to lose. From there, 'with several hundreds of men', he joined Bishop Aethelwine and went to Ely. He, like Morcar and the Bishop, probably intended to seek exile after spending the winter there but was presumably trapped by the Conqueror's men. He, too, was imprisoned after the fall of Ely and, according to Florence of Worcester, was released in 1087. Legend has it that he went overseas to Byzantium as so many Englishmen did and that he was the 'Sigurd Jarl' who commanded the other exiles there in the service of the Emperor. Apart from the fact that he contributed men to the struggle, nothing is known of any action by him while at Ely.

Thorkill of Harringworth

A second leading thegn, and an associate of Hereward, has been identified. He is named in both the *Liber Eliensis* and the *Gesta Herewardi* as Thurcytel or Thurkill, and is considered to be Thorkell the Dane of Harringworth (also termed Thurkill Cild), one of the wealthiest thegns of the East Midlands. His wife has the Danish name Thorgunnr. The *Liber Eliensis* calls Thorkill '*procer*' meaning 'nobleman'. Such a title was used of thegns owning at least forty hides. He is known as 'the Dane' because it was reported that 'he had gone over to the Danes who were his kinsmen' after the Conquest. It is possible but by no means certain that he was the son of Cnut's Earl Thorkell the Tall and certainly the *Ramsey Chronicle* has it that he was of no mean Danish stock. Much of his land was in the area covered by the

Brunneswald, such as Leighton Bromeswold, and it is thought that those lands might well have provided supplies or even safe havens for Hereward and his men, perhaps before as well as after the fight at Ely. His total holding was of over 130 hides and about 140 carucates. He even held some land in Bourne and Rippingale and had other lands in five hundreds in Lincolnshire, which would explain his knowing Hereward. His lands were forfeited to Earl Waltheof after that earl had made his peace with the king.

Of the others, a little is known or can be surmised about a handful, and these are Siward of Maldon, Ordgar the Sheriff, Godric of Corby, Tosti of Davenesse and Rainaldus or Rahenaldus the Steward of Ramsey. There are also several who are said to be Hereward's kinsmen. Little can be said of the others apart from what is recorded in the *Gesta Herewardi* or the *Liber Eliensis*, and that is not much.

Siward 'of Maldon'
He figures in the benefactors list at Ely, where he is said to have been '*socius Herewardi*', that is an associate or companion. He had given fifteen gospel books to Ely (perhaps they came from Peterborough?) and held land in Suffolk, Essex and Cambridgeshire totalling over seventy hides and twenty-five carucates, mainly in Essex. That suggests that he too was '*procer*'.

Ordgar the Sheriff
He is described as one of the '*proceres*' (the word means 'leading figure', even 'noble', and it has been suggested that there were about 100 thegns who could be so described) and an 'illustrious man'. He was Sheriff of Cambridgeshire but was replaced by Picot after 1071. He had been Earl Harold's man, holding land under him as at Sawston and Isleham.

Of the rest of Hereward's men as listed in the sources, little definite can be established, although for some there are tantalising hints of a reality which can only be guessed at. There is Leofric the Deacon, author of the fragments of the older parts of the *Gesta Herewardi*, upon which Richard of Ely seems to have based his version and to which he added the material also found in the *Liber Eliensis*. There is an interesting section in the History of Ramsey, Cap. CI, which relates a story about a '*Leofricis Diaconus*' who made gifts to Ramsey. It is headed '*De Leofrici Diaconi donatione*' and tells how 'Lessius' of Langton who became a deacon in Lindsey gave gifts of land to the abbey when his son became a monk. His son is named as Morkere (Morcar) and the lands were at Witham, Langton, Wipsinton, Merton and Wathingworth. They are not listed as the property of Ramsey in Domesday and so the gift was made after the making of the survey. Wipsinton is probably Wispington, Merton would be Marston and Wathingworth would be Waddingworth; all, with Witham, are in the Lincolnshire Survey, though no entry mentions a Leofric. The Witham is probably Witham-on-the-Hill, which had a church and was associated with Hereward himself.

Another figure who invites fascinating speculations is 'Rahenaldus' or Rainald, said not only to be Hereward's standard-bearer but to have been Steward of Ramsey Abbey. The *Cartulary of Ramsey Abbey* produces an intriguing possibility. In the time of Abbot Ailwin, in the last quarter of the eleventh century, '*R*. [for Ranulph] *Dapifer Regis fratris Ilger*' made a grant to the abbey when he and his wife entered the community. *Ranulph fratris Ilger* was a minor tenant-in-chief recorded as holding lands in several counties.

Among the witnesses to this act two names stand out. The first is 'Rainald Dapifer' who may be the monk 'Rainald' named in another later entry. He is not the Rainald who became abbot in 1114. It cannot be proved that Rainald the Dapifer of the abbey actually was the man called Hereward's standard-bearer, but this entry might well explain where the author of the *Gesta Herewardi* got the idea that Hereward's man was the Steward (dapifer). The other witness is '*Siward filus Toki*', which raises the possibility that this is Asketil's brother and that he had become a monk at Ramsey.

Others whose reality is confirmed are Godric of Corby and Tostig of Davenesse, i.e. Daventry. They are identified in the *Gesta Herewardi* as relatives of Earl Morcar. Godric is said to have been his nephew, not as a son of Earl Edwin, but more likely an otherwise unrecorded son of the eldest son of Earl Aelfgar, Burgheard, who had died in 1062. Tostig is said to be '*cognatus*', a blood relative, of Morcar and to have taken his name in baptism. Morcar might well have been his sponsor then. Tostig could be descended from one of Earl Leofric's three brothers, Northman, Godwin and Edwin (and one of these three was probably the father of Abbot Leofric of Peterborough who was Leofric's nephew). Such relationships explain the prominence given to these two by the author of the *Gesta Herewardi*.

Then there are those identified as relatives of Hereward himself, that is his cousins. These include the two Siwards, Rufus and Albus, the red and the blond, who accompanied him in his exile. As they are paternal cousins they should be seen as sons of either Siward or Siric, brothers of Asketil. A Siward Rufus held land in Northorpe Hundred in 1086. Other cousins are named as Godwin Gille, Geri, and the twins Auti and Duti, and two others are '*cognatus*', Winter and Liveret. These might all be the sons of the members of the extended family descended from Auti the Moneyer.

All the others are even more shadowy, such as Turbentinus, said to be '*pronepos*', literally great-grandson of Eadgar. This cannot mean the Aetheling, but it is not impossible that he might just be a descendant of one of King Aethelraede's sons, and Aethelraede was son to King Eadgar. The Confessor was grandson to Eadgar, so a great-grandson is not outside the bounds of possibility.

It has been suggested that Wulfwine Cild was another supporter, though he is not listed among Hereward's men nor said to have been at Ely, but he lost his lands after 1071 because they turn up in the hands of Countess Judith, Earl Waltheof's widow, and Waltheof was given most of the lands of those implicated in the resistance at Ely. Judith also had an estate at Daventry.

One confusion can be cleared up. The opening section of the *Gesta Herewardi* lists a number of Hereward's men as still living when the text was written. It lists '*Siwate* (Siward) *frater, Broter de Sancto Edmundo*' and others. This first entry represents one man, not two as in some transcriptions. It identifies Brother Siward of Bury St Edmunds; the '*broter*' is 'brother' and translated into English the less familiar Latin of '*frater*'. An interesting individual is Acere Vasus or 'the Hard', of whom it is said that his father owned 'the tower of the city', that is Lincoln. That tower was later under the control of Countess Lucy, formerly wife of Ivo Taillebois, daughter of Thorold of Lincoln and probably, through her mother, granddaughter of William Malet. She was not, as legend states, sister to Edwin and Morcar. Lucy's family seem to have had custody of the tower before her, as they did after her. What connection they might have to Acere Vasus cannot be established.

Some of the other men have nicknames. There was Wluric Rahere, that is, Hraga – the heron – who came from Wroxham bridge (Norfolk) who is described as 'ardea', which poetically indicates 'high in the air'. Perhaps he was a stilt man. Others include Leofwine

Prat, which means crafty; Thrachitell (Thorketil) the boy
or child; Thurstan Juvenis, the young; Lewine (Leofwine)
Mone, the sickle, who fought using one; and Martin
Lightfoot, Hereward's constant companion and servant
in Flanders. The rest can only be listed:

Wluncas the Black
Wlfric White
Wluric Grugan
Leofric the Black
Starcolf
Hogor the Cook
Gaenoch
Ylard
Alveriz*
Grugan*
Saiswold*
Azecier*
Ailward the Chaplain
Vllicus (=bailiff) of Drayton
Matelgar
Toste of Rothwell
Godwin of Rothwell
Osbern
Alsinus
Broher
Alutas Grugan
Hugo the Norman, priest
Wluric White
Wenotus

*all in Gaimar, along with Geri and Winter.

Appendix 2: Hereward's Principal Opponents

Abbot Turold of Peterborough

This former monk of Fécamp who had enjoyed a brief period as Abbot of Malmesbury, though his monks there did not, was appointed to Peterborough on the death of Abbot Brand. That he was a Norman would in itself have been enough to provoke Hereward; that he replaced his uncle, Abbot Brand, no doubt added insult to injury. William of Malmesbury reported that this man Turold so loved playing the soldier that King William remarked that he might as well be given someone to fight.

He was impatient to take up his new appointment, and arrived in the area near Stamford in Lincolnshire with 160 knights, a small army, indicating perhaps that resistance to his appointment was expected. News of his arrival spread like wildfire, and tenants of the abbey of Peterborough, who included Hereward, sent word to the Danes offering to guide them in an attack on the monastery in order to seize its treasures so that they might not fall into Norman hands. As related earlier, Hereward and his men assisted the Danes in stripping the monastery. Turold on arrival found a ruined abbey, empty of monks. However, no permanent harm had been done and within a few days normal monastic services were resumed as most of the monks gradually returned.

The account of these events is most fully recorded by Hugh Candidus, who relates how Turold exploited the resources of Peterborough, granting out lands to his relatives and stipendiary knights. That his relatives benefited can be confirmed: a Geoffrey Infans, nephew of the abbot, and Roger Infans, another probable nephew, both held abbey lands, but the idea that Hugh d'Envermeu was a relative is false. (Hugh's brother was another Turold, Bishop of Bayeux, not the Abbot of Peterborough.) The granting of fiefs became necessary after King William imposed a burden of military service on the abbey, requiring the service of sixty knights. The sources also maintain that the granting of fiefs was intended to reward Turold's men for protecting him against Hereward. Turold is also reported by Hugh Candidus' continuator to have built a motte and bailey castle in the precincts with which to defend the abbey, which in his day was called 'Mount Turold'. The motte is still there in the Prior's Garden.

Other stories are less easy to pin down. Some sources maintain that Turold, and possibly also Ivo Taillebois who is reported to have joined with him in seeking to capture Hereward, became a prisoner of the outlaws and was released on Hereward's orders, by Siward the White, for the impossible ransom of 30,000 marks of silver (or £30,000 in another version) and that this followed Hereward's attack on Stamford during the time he spent in the Brunneswald after escaping from Ely. A ransom of 300 marks would be more credible; perhaps the sum was magnified in the telling of the tale. No totally reliable source reports this story and it may only be a myth based on an inconclusive skirmish between Turold and Ivo on one side and Hereward and his men on the other. It may relate to the other tale that Hereward confronted Turold when he first arrived and warned him to stay away from Peterborough.

William Malet

Although the *Gesta Herewardi* and other sources do not name William Malet as present during the blockade of Ely, it is accepted that he died at Ely. There are charters dated as being written 'when William Malet went into the marshes' (and obviously, did not return!). Certainly

Robert Malet took over his lands in 1071 and Domesday entries about these lands record them as held 'when he went away on the king's service'.

He was from Graville-Sainte-Honorine near Le Havre and was almost certainly in England before the Conquest, and married Esilia, daughter of another baron, Miles Crispin. William and his wife had several daughters. The eldest, Beatrice, married William d'Arques, another married Alfred of Lincoln, and a third married Thorold the Sheriff. Lucy 'the Countess', wife of Ivo Taillebois, was his granddaughter.

He is said to have been ordered to bury King Harold in an unmarked grave on the shore at Hastings (though the body was recovered by his mother and buried at Waltham) and he may have led the group of knights who gave Harold the coup de grâce towards the end of the battle. He acquired the estates of Eadric of Laxfield and was made sheriff and a castellan at York where he was besieged and captured, with his family. He also acquired large estates in Holderness.

He was succeeded by his son Robert, who inherited lands, his castle at Eye in Suffolk and his whole 'honour'. Robert Malet joined with William de Warenne and others, according to the *Gesta Herewardi*, in obtaining Hereward's alleged imprisonment at Bedford.

Ivo Taillebois

That he was at Ely is recorded in the sources. It was his idea to employ a 'pythoness' or witch to curse the defenders and so sap their will to resist. He is associated with Turold in stories of conflicts with Hereward and his men after their escape from Ely, and possibly earlier, at the time Turold first came to Peterborough.

Ivo Taillebois (the name means 'Cut-bush') held most of his land in Lincolnshire where he was sheriff, and married

Lucy, daughter of Thorold of Lincoln, and a granddaughter
of William Malet. He is pictured in the *History of Crowland*
by Ingulf as the determined enemy of that abbey and a
cruel and rapacious baron.

William de Warenne

This baron, one of the richest in England, was of a family
with lands and connections in Flanders and he married
Gundrada (the Conqueror's step-daughter), sister of
Frederick of Oosterzele-Scheldewindeke whose estates in
England passed to his brother-in-law after his death (see
below) at the hands of Hereward. It was perhaps that
death which made de Warenne the determined enemy of
Hereward, but that they were opponents earlier than that
is probable. William was one of the king's closest advisers
and is shown in this role in both the *Gesta Herewardi* and
the *Liber Eliensis* where he criticises the knight Deda for
his too-flattering account of Hereward, after his sojourn as
a prisoner on the Isle. With Robert Malet he is described as
still an enemy of Hereward even after Hereward's alleged
reconciliation to the king.

As a result of the marriage, William's sons inherited the
role of hereditary advocates of St Bertin at St Omer held by
Frederick, as well as land in the Ardres-Guines county. It is
quite probable that William de Warenne had encountered
Hereward in Flanders and indeed, during the encounter
between them described in the *Gesta Herewardi*, when
Hereward was on his way to Ely from Bardney, de Warenne
accuses Hereward of having robbed his superiors of some
of the spoils of the campaign in Scaldemariland.

Frederick of Oosterzele-Scheldewindeke

Brother-in-law of William de Warenne, he was ambushed and
killed by Hereward and his men. The *Gesta Herewardi* puts

this during Hereward's brief first return to England after the Conquest and this may be dated to 1068, as Frederick could well have come to England with his brother Gerbod II, Earl of Chester from 1067 to 1071 (also known as Gerbod of St Omer or Flandrensis). The brothers had many connections with St Omer, and the abbey of St Bertin, of which they were hereditary advocates and, although the exact circumstances are not recorded, it is probable that the reasons for his assassination by Hereward lie in some encounter between them in Flanders. Perhaps Frederick was one of those who were jealous of his success in Scaldemariland.

Richard fitzGilbert

This great baron, named in the *Liber Eliensis* as 'Gilbert of Clare', was head of the widespread Clare family and was son to Count Gilbert of Brionne (grandson of Duke Richard I). His seat in England was at Clare in Suffolk, with another great centre at Tunbridge in Kent. In the *Liber Eliensis* he is an adviser to King William, who upbraids the monks of Ely for dining in the refectory instead of welcoming the king, and so brings about the levying of a fine of 700 silver marks upon them so that they may regain the king's favour. He was, with William de Warenne, one of those who barred Earl Ralph Guader's way and prevented his joining up with Roger of Hereford during their rebellion. With Warenne he was one of the eleven richest barons in England and, with him, was one of the king's inner circle. Baldwin fitzGilbert, who married the daughter of Richard de Rullos and so acquired some of the estates once held by Hereward, was his grandson.

Ogier the Breton

Ogier, son of Ungomar, received some of the lands, notably at Rippingale and Ringstone, Laughton, Aslackby and

Avethorpe, once held by Hereward. He was Lord of Bourne,
a circumstance which accounts for the later impression that
Hereward had been Lord of Bourne and that his father was
Leofric of Bourne, according to the *Gesta Herewardi* and
Pseudo-Ingulf. Bourne in fact belonged to Morcar, which
probably explains the equally erroneous idea that Leofric
of Bourne was Leofric of Mercia.

Ogier was succeeded by his son Roger as holder of the 'fief
of Bourne' and it later became part of the various parcels
of land gathered up by Henry I to form the 'honour' of
Bourne granted to Baldwin fitzGilbert who had acquired
the lordship along with the daughter of Richard 'de Rullos',
brother of William who was Lord of Bourne before him. The
exact way in which these lands passed from Ogier to the
de Rullos brothers is unknown, although it involves Hugh
d'Envermeu. The easy solution, adopted by Ingulf, was to
claim that Hugh had married Hereward's daughter, which
leads some to conclude that Ogier must have married her
mother. But this can be shown to be both false and baseless.
If Ogier's son had no issue, then the manor could have been
acquired by Hugh for money, probably from William Rufus
or Henry I.

As he had been given lands which had once belonged to
Hereward, the latter's hostility to Ogier is easily explained.
In both Gaimar (who calls him '*Ogger*') and in the *Gesta
Herewardi*, Hereward and Ogier fight.

Tables

Table 1
Lands of Hereward

Manor	Geld Rating	Value TRE	Owner 1086
Laughton	4 bovates	40 shillings	Ogier le Breton
Laughton	1 carucate	–	Ogier
Aslackby & Avethorpe	6 bovates	–	Ogier
Rippingale	3 carucates	40s	Ogier
Ringstone	1 carucate	–	Ogier
Ringstone with Rippingale	1 carucate	–	Ogier
Witham on the Hill etc.	12 bovates	40s	Peterborough Abbey
Berewick	4 bovates	5s 4d	Peterborough Abbey
Barholme with Stowe	1 carucate	20s	Peterborough Abbey
Soke as above	4.5 bovates	–	Peterborough Abbey
Sokeland of Stowe	1 carucate	–	Asfort
Soke in Stowe	2 bovates	3s	Godfrey
Totals	12 carucates	£7 8s 4d	–

Berewicks and Sokes dependent upon manors have had their value included in that of the relevant manor.

TRE = *Tempus Regis Edwardi*, i.e. in the time of King Edward.

Table 2
Lands of Asketil the King's Thegn

Lincolnshire

Manor	Geld Rating	Value	1086 Holder
Scotter	8 carucates	£11	Peterborough Abbey
Scotton	6 carucates	£5	Peterborough Abbey
'Raventhorpe'	2 carucates	£6	Peterborough Abbey
Walton	6 car., 5 bovates	£6	Peterborough Abbey
Appleby & Risby	3 bovates	£1	Peterborough Abbey

Sokes

Haythby (1)	2 bovates	–	Peterborough Abbey
Northope	1 carucate	–	Peterborough Abbey
Scotterthorpe	3 carucates	–	Peterborough Abbey
Haythby (2)	–	–	Peterborough Abbey

Berewicks

Alkborough	1 carucate	–	Peterborough Abbey
Spilsby	6 carucates	£1	Durham Cathedral
Firsby	3 car., 5 bovates	£3	Odo of Bayeux
South Willingham	6.5 bovates	£1	Odo of Bayeux
Cockerington	3 car., 1 bovate	£3	Odo of Bayeux
Withcall	3.5 carucates	£4	Odo of Bayeux
Stewton	3 bovates	£1	Odo of Bayeux
Aby	14 bovates	£3	Odo of Bayeux

Sokes

Alvingham	4 bov. + 2 parts	–	Odo of Bayeux
Strubby	1 car., 2 bovates	–	Odo of Bayeux
Kexby	3 car., 3.5 bov.	£2	Colsuen of Lincoln
Ashby	3.5 carucates	£2 10s	Colsuen of Lincoln
Saxby	2.5 carucates	£2	Eudo fitz Spirewic
Barholme	1 carucate	£1	Godfrey de Cambrai

Stowe	1.5 carucates	2s	Godfrey de Cambrai
Fulstowe	14 bovates	£5	Robert Despencer
Croxton	6 bovates	£2	Roger de Poitou
Kirmington	4 bovates	£1	Count Alan of Richmond
Totals	62 car., 2 bov.	£60 12s	

Hertfordshire

Ware	24 hides	£50	Hugh de Grandmesnil
Brent	2.5 hides	£15	Bishop of London
Brent	3 hides, 1 vir.	£6	Bishop of London
Westmill	4 hides, 3 vir.	£10	Ralph de Tosny
Sacombe	3 virgates	15s	Hardwin de Scales
Wallington	1.5 hides	30s	Hardwin de Scales

Bedfordshire

Stotfold	15 hides	£20	Hugh de Beauchamp
Willington	10 hides	£6	Hugh de Beauchamp
Keysoe	4 hides, 3 vir.	£5	Hugh de Beauchamp
Keysoe	1 hide	–	Hugh de Beauchamp
Putnoe	4 hides	£2	Hugh de Beauchamp
Channel's End	5 hides	£7	Hugh de Beauchamp
Channel's End	0.5 hide	2s	Hugh de Beauchamp
Cople	3 virgates	6s	Hugh de Beauchamp
Bletsoe	2.5 hides	£3	Hugh de Beauchamp
Wyboston	0.5 virgate	2s	Hugh de Beauchamp
Henlow	1 hide, 3 vir.	30s	Hugh de Beauchamp
Henlowe	1 hide	23s	Hugh + 2 sokemen
Holme	1 virgate	3s	Hugh + 1 sokeman
Goldington	3 hides	£3	Hugh + Almaer
Maulden	0.5 virgate	12s	Hugh + Godwine
Hockliffe	10 hides	£12	Widow of Ralph Taillebois
Colmworth	5 hides	£5	Hugh de Beauchamp

Kent

Beckenham	2 sulungs	£9	Odo of Bayeux

| Howbury | 1 sulung | £3 | Odo of Bayeux |
| Wricklesworth | 1 sulung | £7 | Odo of Bayeux |

Northamptonshire

Lower	1 hide	30s	Earl Hugh Boddington
Byfield	8 hides	£8	Earl Hugh
Trafford	1 hide, 1 vir.	30s	Hugh's men
Marston	4 hides	£10	Hugh's men
Radstone	2 hides	£5	Hugh's men
Middleton	1 hide	£3	Hugh's men
Cheney			
Slapton	4 hides	£3	Hugh's men
Yelvertoft	2 hides 1 vir.	£1	Hugh's men

Nottinghamshire

| West | 4 bovates | £2 | De Busli Markham |

Yorkshire

Great Ayton	2 carucates	10s	Robert Malet
Scawton	3 carucates	10s	Robert Malet
Thormanby	4 carucates	10s	Robert Malet
'Bernebi'	4 carucates	waste	Robert Malet
'Horenbodebi'	2 car., 2 bov.	waste	Robert Malet
Murton	6 carucates	waste	Robert Malet
Dale Town	1.5 carucates	waste	Robert Malet
Thornton le Clay	2 carucates	waste	Robert Malet
East Carlton	3 carucates	waste	Robert Malet

Totals	93 hides, 3 vir.	£105.18s	
	28 car., 2 bov.	£3.10s	
	9 sulungs	£19	

Maps and Genealogical Tables

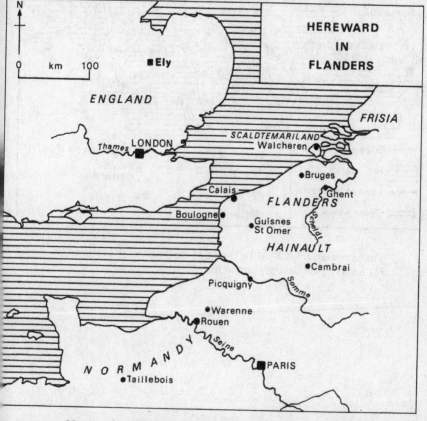

Hereward in Flanders. © Mike Young, by kind permission of
The Ely Society Publications Committee.

The campaign at Ely. © Mike Young, by kind permission of The
Ely Society Publications Committee.

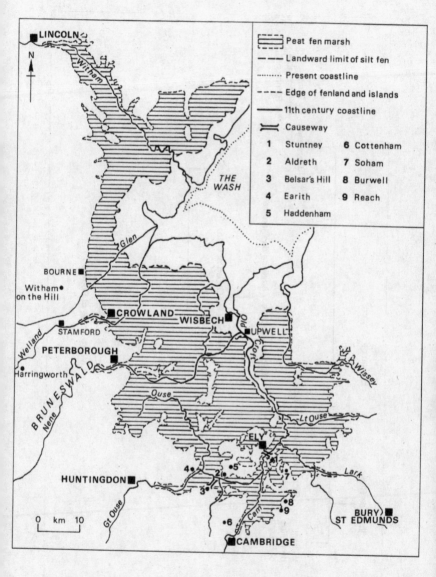

The Fens in the time of Hereward. © Mike Young, by kind
permission of The Ely Society Publications Committee.

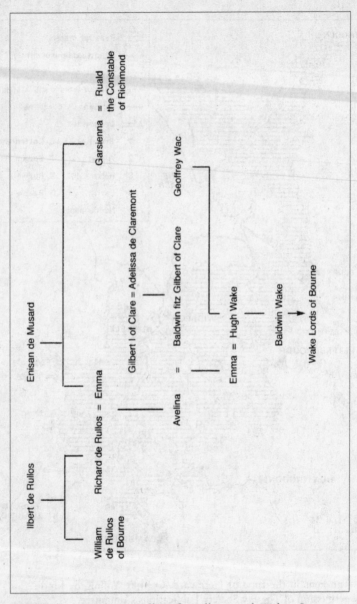

The descent of De Rullos, fitzGilbert and Wake. ©
Christina Rex.

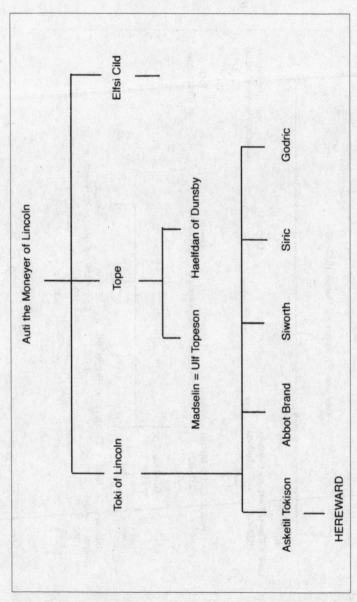

The family of Abbot Brand. © Christina Rex.

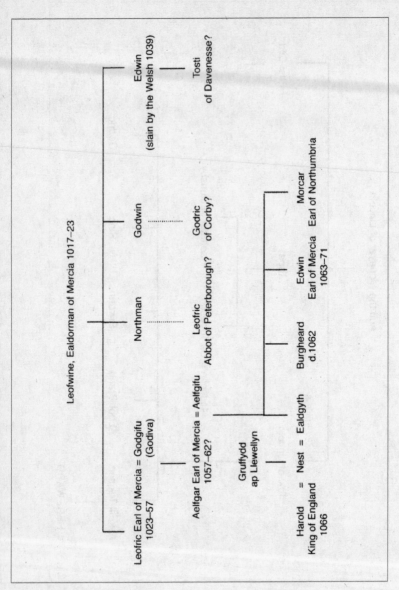

The House of Leofric, Earl of Mercia. © Christina Rex.

Bibliography

Primary Sources

Chronicles, Narratives and Other Documentary Sources

Arnold, T. (ed.), *Historia Anglorum*, Henry of Huntingdon.
London, 1879. Archdeacon Henry adapted earlier sources,
writing shortly before 1150.

Bell, A. (ed.), *L'Estorie des Engles*, Geoffrey Gaimar. Anglo-
Norman Text Society, Oxford, 1960. He wrote this Norman
French poem before 1140 for his patroness, Constance, wife
of Ralf fitzGilbert. It is part fact and part romantic fiction.

Blake, E. O. (ed.), *Liber Eliensis*. London, 1962. Book Two
of this work was compiled at Ely, probably by the monk
Richard of Ely, before 1174, and contains extended extracts
from an earlier version of the *Gesta Herewardi* with matter
from other sources between the extracts.

Cartularium Monasterii de Rameseia. Rolls Series, 1884. A
mid-twelfth-century work with information about Leofric
the Deacon and Rahenaldus, Hereward's standard-bearer.

Chibnall, M. (ed. & trans.), *The Ecclesiastical History*,
Ordericus Vitalis. Oxford, 1969–80. Orderic, whose English
name was Vital, was brought up in Shropshire. He wrote a
general history of both England and Normandy while at S.
Evroul between 1123 and 1141.

Chronicle of Ramsey Abbey. Rolls Series, 1884. From Ramsey

Abbey in the mid-twelfth century, this work supplements the Cartulary.

Davis, H. W. C. (ed.), *Regesta Regum Anglo-Normannorum*. Vol. 1: Oxford, 1913.

Vol. 2 (ed. Johnson, C. & Cronne, H. A.): Oxford, 1956. A useful calendar of the writs of the early Norman kings.

Douglas, D. & Greenaway, G. W. (eds), *English Historical Documents*. Vol. 2, 1042–1189. London, 1953. This is a collection of the major sources on all aspects of the post-Conquest period from 1042 to 1189.

Foster, C. W. & Longley, T. (eds), *Lincolnshire Domesday and the Lindsey Survey*. Lincoln Record Society, 1924. A detailed edition of the Domesday entries for Lincolnshire.

Garmonsway, G. N. (trans.), *Anglo-Saxon Chronicle*. London, 1953. A complete translation of all manuscript versions of the chronicles. It contains the text of the *Worcester Chronicle* (D) from the year 1100 or thereabouts and the *Peterborough Chronicle* (E) based on a text from Canterbury to which much local information was added for the period after 1066. It was written at Peterborough after 1109.

Hardy, T. D. & Martin, C. T. (eds), *Gesta Herewardi*. Rolls Series, London, 1888. The authoritative edition, with translation, of the thirteenth-century text of the *Gesta Herewardi*.

Hunter, J. (ed.), *Pipe Roll 31 Henry I*. Record Commission, London, 1833. This is the earliest text of the Pipe Roll compiled by the King's Exchequer and the only example surviving from the reign of Henry I.

Martin, J., *Cartularies and Registers of Peterborough Abbey*. Northants. Rec. Soc. Xxviii, 1978. A useful review of the available sources from Peterborough Abbey.

Mellows, W. T. (ed.), *The Chronicle of Hugh Candidus*. Oxford, 1941. Incorporates the *Annales Burgo-Spaldenses*. Hugh Candidus wrote at Peterborough Abbey in the mid-twelfth century and his work contains the Peterborough traditions about Hereward. This edition also contains extracts relating to Hereward from the fourteenth-century annals which were the first written source to call him 'le Wake'.

Paris, Matthew, *Chronica Majora*. Rolls Series. This is a thirteenth-century work from the greatest of medieval historians, with many useful traditions from the abbey of St Albans where he wrote his major works.

Robertson, A. J. (ed. & trans.), *The Laws of the Kings of England from Edmund to Henry I*. Cambridge, 1925. An edition of Anglo-Saxon laws from Cnut the Great to Henry I.

Roffe, D., *Descriptio Terrarum* of Peterborough Abbey. Bull. Inst. Hist. Res. LXV No. 156, 1992. This is a study of the late eleventh-century list of the lands of the abbey, showing how various estates passed down from one holder to another.

Sparke, J., *Annales Burgo-Spaldenses* in *Historiae Anglicanae Scriptores*. London, 1723. The only extant edition of these annals of the fourteenth century which contain traditions about Hereward.

Stevenson, J. (ed. & trans.), *Chronicon ex Chronicis*, Florence of Worcester. London, 1853. This author wrote his 'History of Histories' at Worcester, probably between 1082 and 1130, basing it on the *Chronicle of Marianus Scotus* and a version of the *Anglo-Saxon Chronicle* which is no longer extant.

Stevenson, J. (ed. & trans.), *Historia Croylandensis*, Ingulf. London, 1854. This is a fabricated work of the fourteenth century, claiming to be the work of Ingulf who was abbot of Crowland in William Rufus' time. He used much genuine material, including a text of the *Gesta Herewardi* or very similar document, but he makes many errors arising from ignorance of the nature of his sources and makes up his own accounts where he has no source to draw on.

Stevenson, J. (ed. & trans.), *L'Estorie des Engles*, Geoffrey Gaimar. London, 1854. A useful but not entirely accurate translation of this work.

Stevenson, J. (trans.), *Liber de Hyda*. London, 1854. A translation of this curious and much-disputed work of uncertain date and provenance.

Stubbs, W., *Select Charters*, Eighth Ed. Oxford, 1900. A useful collection of sources not readily available elsewhere.

Swaffham, Robert of, *De Gestis Herewardi*, in Peterborough M.S.1., Cambridge University Library. This is the original text from the thirteenth century, in Robert of Swaffham's Register.

Sweeting, Revd W. D. (trans.) & Miller, S. H. (ed.), *De Gestis Herewardi Saxonis*. Peterborough, 1895. A useful edition of the text of the *Gesta Herewardi*, with translation.

Williams, A. & Martin, G. H. (ed. & trans.), *Domesday Book*. London, 2002. A valuable one-volume translation of Domesday Book.

Secondary Sources

Astbury, A. K., *The Black Fens*. Cambridge, 1958. A valuable account of the nature, history and topography of the Fens.

Bailey, M. W., *Lincolnshire and the Fens*. London, 1952. Useful material about Fenland waterways.

Barlow, F., *Edward the Confessor*. London, 1970. One of the best available biographies of the Confessor.

Barlow, F., *The English Church, 1066–1154*. London, 1979. A good account of the effects of the Conquest on the Church.

Bates, D., *William the Conqueror*. Tempus, 2004. A sound if rather routine biography of the Conqueror.

Bennett, M., *Campaigns of the Norman Conquest*. Osprey, 2001. Contains a useful discussion of the Ely Campaign by a military historian.

Bennett, M., 'The Conqueror faces a fight back', *History Magazine* Vol. 3 No. 1 Jan., 2002. A popular version of the views in his book.

Bevis, T., *Hereward of the Fens* (trans. *De Gestis Herewardi Saxonis*). March, Cambs., 1956. A rather pedestrian edition, widely available in the Fens, marred by errors of translation.

Blair, P. H., *An Introduction to Anglo-Saxon England.* Cambridge, 1956. A useful account of the nature and institutions of pre-Conquest England.

Bosworth & Toller, *Anglo-Saxon Dictionary.* 1898. An old-fashioned but sound dictionary.

Cambridgeshire and Huntingdonshire Archaeological Society Transactions, Vol. 1. Contains valuable archaeological information.

Cavill, P., *Vikings: Fear and Faith in Anglo-Saxon England.* Harper Collins, 2001. Provides good background on the Viking Age.

Chadwick, H. M., *Studies in Anglo-Saxon Institutions.* New York, 1963. A most authoritative account of Anglo-Saxon institutions.

Chapman, A. E., *For Hereward and Freedom.* Fenland Press, 1933. This novel, like others of its kind, plays fast and loose with the facts.

Ciggaar, K. N., 'Byzantine Marginalia to the Norman Conquest', *Anglo-Norman Studies* IX, 1986. Comments on the fare and identity of Siward Barn and the Knight Deda.

Clemoes, P., *The Anglo-Saxons.* London, 1950. A sound survey of the Anglo-Saxon period.

Complete Peerage. New Edition, Vol. XII Part 2. Useful for its account of the Wake barony of Bourne.

Coneybeare, E., *Highways and Byways in Cambridgeshire and Ely.* London, 1910. Some useful topographical hints.

Coss, P., *The Knight in Medieval England 1000–1400.* Stroud, 1996. Casts valuable light on the development and nature of knighthood.

Darby, H. C., *Medieval Fenland.* Newton Abbot, 1949. A sound study of the geography and topography of the fens in the Middle Ages.

Darby, H. C., *The Changing Fenland.* 1983. Deals with the changes in river systems.

Davis, H. W. C., *England under the Normans and Angevins 1066–1172.* London, 1949. Summarises the older view of the Hereward story and lists the main sources for it.

Davis, R. H. C., *Alfred the Great to Stephen*. 1991. A good general survey of the period.

De Brouard, M., *Guillaume le Conquerant*. Caen, 1984. A sound French view of the Conqueror and his rise.

Dictionary of National Biography. Articles on Hereward and others. Good general articles on the personalities involved in the story of Hereward, if now rather out-of-date.

Douglas, D. C., *William the Conqueror*. London, 1964. Still the most detailed account of the Conqueror's career.

Douglas, D. C., *Feudal Documents from the Abbey of Bury St Edmunds*. 1932 An edition of Abbot Baldwin's collection of documents, which casts light on some of his men.

Dring, W. E., *The Fenland Story*. Cambs. & Ely Educ. Comm., 1967. Useful impressions of the changing nature of the Fens and their watercourses.

Farrer, C. F., *Ouse's Silent Tide*. Bedford, 1921. Describes the history of the Ouse and the changes which have occurred through the ages.

Fenland Notes and Queries III, 1895–97 & 1901–03. Many curious articles on matters archaeological.

Fleming, R., *Kings and Lords in Conquest England*. Cambridge, 1991. Looks at the nature of land holding, especially before as well as after the Conquest.

Fleming, R., 'Domesday Book and the Tenurial Revolution', *A.N.S.* IX, 1986. Contributes to the ongoing debate on this problem.

Fowler, G., 'Fenland Waterways', *Cambs. Antiquarian Society Proceedings*, No. xxxiii, 1931–32. Another contribution to the history of changes in the Fenland waterways.

Freeman, E. A., *The History of the Norman Conquest of England*. 6 Vols. Oxford, 1867–79. This monumental Victorian study still contains many useful insights.

Ganshof, F. L., *Feudalism*. London, 1961. A handy account of the nature of feudalism, especially the rites of homage and investiture.

Gillingham, J., 'Thegns and Knights in eleventh century England; Who was then the gentleman?', *Royal Historical*

Society Transactions, Sixth Series, No. V, 1996. Contributes to the debate on the problem of continuity between thegns and knights.

Gordon, P., *The Wakes of Northamptonshire*. Northants. C. C., 1992. A well-researched account of the Wake family, showing the difficulty of tracing it back beyond Baldwin fitzGilbert.

Hall, D. & Coles, J., *Fenland Survey*. English Heritage, 1994. A mine of information about Fenland topography.

Harper, C. G., *The Cambridge, Ely and King's Lynn Road*. Chapman & Hall, 1902. Some curious and interesting comments on Fenland history.

Hart, C. R., 'Hereward "the Wake" and His Companions', in *The Danelaw*. Hambledon Press, 1992. Sets Hereward in his Fenland background and identifies some of his men.

Hart, C. R., *Early Charters of Eastern England*. Leicester, 1966. Contains the charters relating to Abbot Brand and Peterborough Abbey.

Hart, C. R., *Early Charters of Northern England and the North Midlands*. Leicester, 1975. A useful survey of the available documents.

Hart, C. R., 'Hereward', *C.A.S. Proc.*, 1974. The first draft of what became the account of Hereward in *The Danelaw*.

Hart, C. R., 'Land Tenure in Cambridgeshire on the Eve of the Norman Conquest', *C.A.S. Proc.* lxxxiv, 1995. Reviews the situation in Cambridgeshire and identifies some land holders.

Harward, Lt-Gen. T. N., *Hereward the Saxon Patriot*. Wisbech, 1896. A most extraordinary work with an eccentric mix of fact and fiction. It attacks the Wake claims and asserts the Lt-General's own claim to be a descendant of Hereward. He even hints that the founder of Harvard University was a descendant!

Hayward, J., 'Hereward the Outlaw', *Journal of Medieval History* 14, 1988. Looks at the *Gesta* in its literary setting and summarises the state of research up to 1988.

Hayward, P., 'Translation Narratives in Post-Conquest Hagiography and the English Resistance', *A.N.S.* XXI, 1995. Casts light on the clerical dimension in English attitudes to the Conquest.

Head, V., *Hereward*. A. Sutton, 1995. An interesting but eventually disappointing review of the Hereward legend which peters out into irrelevant genealogical matters.

Higham, N. J., *The Death of Anglo-Saxon England*. 1997. An interesting account of the last years of the pre-Conquest English State.

Hill, J. W. F., *Medieval Lincoln*. Cambridge, 1948. A very useful account of Lincoln in the Norman period.

Hinde, T. (ed.), *Domesday Book, England's Heritage Then and Now*. London, 1985. A readable summary of the entries in Domesday Book for each county.

Hole, C., *English Folk Heroes*. Batsford, 1948. Hereward as a legendary figure.

Hooker, F. H., *The Stuntney Book*. 1984–86. A local study of a Fenland village.

Hudson, J., 'Essential Histories; the Norman Conquest', *BBC History Magazine* Vol. 4 No. 1, Jan. 2003. Exactly what it claims to be: a summary of essential facts.

Jerrold, D., *An Introduction to the History of England*. London, 1949. A good if somewhat idiosyncratic general survey.

John, E., *Reassessing Anglo-Saxon England*. Manchester University Press, 1996. Questions some of the more facile assumptions about this period.

Keats-Rowan, K. S. B., *Domesday People*. Woodbridge, 1999. A 'who was who' of Domesday Book.

Keats-Rowan, K. S. B., *Domesday Descendants*. Woodbridge, 2002. Accomplishes the same task for their successors.

Kenney, J. & Oswald, A., 'Belsar's Hill, Willingham'. *C.A.S. Proc.* lxxxiv, 1995. The archaeology of this site.

King, E., *Peterborough Abbey 1086–1310*. Cambridge, 1973. A well-researched study of the abbey's history.

King, E., *Descriptio Terrarum of Peterborough Abbey* in *Northampton Past and Present*, Vol. V No. 3, 1979.

Edits a document which throws light on Abbot Turold's enfeoffments.

Kingsley, Charles, *Hereward the Wake*. London, 1867. Victorian fictionalisation of Hereward's story but with a good historical introduction. For an exciting modern fictionalisation of the Hereward subject, see James Wilde's Hereward trilogy.

Lawson, M. K., *Cnut; the Danes in England in the Early Eleventh Century*. Longman, 1993. A sound account of Cnut's reign and its effects.

Lethbridge, T. C., articles in *C.A.S. Proc. 1931–35, 1924, 1944*. Various attempts to solve the puzzle of the Conqueror's route in attacking Ely.

Lethbridge, T. C., *Merlin's Island*. London, 1948. Summarises the available archaeological clues about the attack on Ely.

Loyn, H. R., *Anglo-Saxon England and the Norman Conquest*. London, 1962. A good modern account of the period.

Loyn, H. R., *The Governance of Anglo-Saxon England 500–1087*. London. A useful survey of the development of governmental institutions.

Lyons, D. & Lyons, S., *Magna Brittania*. Cambridgeshire, 1808. Contains much curious information.

MacFarlane, C., *The Camp of Refuge*. Constable, 1897. This Victorian work of fiction bears little relation to the facts but the historical introduction is very useful.

Maitland, F. W., *Domesday Book and Beyond*. Cambridge, 1907. A still fascinating study of what Domesday Book can tell us about pre-Conquest England.

Matthew, D. J. A., *The Norman Conquest*, London, 1966. A readable history of the various stages of the Conquest.

Miller, E., *The Abbey and Bishopric of Ely*. Cambridge, 1951. A good survey of the abbey's history.

Oman, Sir Charles, *England Before the Norman Conquest*. London, 1921. A good if old-fashioned history which provides a readable introduction to the subject.

Oosthuizen, S., *Cambridgeshire from the Air*. Univ. of Cambridge, 1996. An illuminating collection of aerial photographs.

Page, F. M., *The estates of Crowland abbey*. Cambridge, 1934. Summarises Crowland's land holdings.

Petty, P. & M., *The Peoples' Ford*. 1981. A study of this village's history by a noted local historian.

Prestwich, J. O., 'Anglo-Norman Feudalism and the Problem of Continuity', *Past and Present* No. 26, 1963. An interesting contribution to this controversial topic.

Prestwich, M., 'Miles in Armis Strenuis; the Knight at War', *R.H.S. Trans.* Sixth Series, No. V. Casts light on Hereward's status and claims in the twelfth century that he was a knight.

Raban, S., 'Estates of Thorney and Crowland', *Cambridge Occasional Papers* 7, 1977. Describes the land holdings of these two Fenland monasteries.

Roffe, D., 'From Thegnage to Barony; Sake and Soke, Title and Tenants-in-Chief', *A.N.S.* XII, 1989. Studies the process of transition from English to Norman land holding.

Roffe, D., 'Hereward the Wake and the Barony of Bourne', *Lincolnshire History and Archaeology*, Vol. 29, 1994. Establishes Hereward's aristocratic status and considers theories about his descendants.

Round, J. H., *Feudal England*. London, 1909.

Round, J. H., *Peerage and Pedigree*. 1910.

Round, J. H., *Studies in Peerage and Family History*. 1901. Articles in these works contribute to research about the families of the post-Conquest period, including that of Wales, whose connection with Hereward is questioned.

Sanders, I. J., *English Baronies; a Study of their Origin and Descent, 1086–1327*. Oxford, 1960. The best study of the development of post-Conquest baronies.

Sayles, G. O., *The Medieval Foundations of England*. London, 1948. Studies English institutions and their development.

'Scientific Survey of the Cambridge District', *Brit. Assoc.* 1938. Useful genealogical and archaeological survey.

Skeat, W., *Place Names of Cambridgeshire*. Cambridge, 1911. Informative study of the etymology of place names.

Snelson, P. (ed.), *Along the Cam and the Great Ouse*. Cambs. Libraries Pub., 1995. More useful data on changes in river flow.

Stafford, P., *Unification and Conquest*. London, 1989. Interesting re-evaluation of established theories.

Stenton, F. M., *Anglo-Saxon England*. Oxford, 1971. Still the best all-round study of Anglo-Saxon England.

Stenton, F. M., *First Century of English Feudalism 1066–1166*. Oxford, 1932. The best survey of the introduction of feudalism in England.

Summers, D., *The Great Ouse*. 1973. Studies the Great Ouse from source to estuary.

Swanton, M., *Three Lives of the Last Englishmen*. London, 1984. Contains a useful if limited translation of the *Gesta Herewardi*.

Taylor, A., *Anglo-Saxon Cambridgeshire*. Cambridge, 1978.

Taylor, A., *Archaeology of South-East Cambridgeshire and Fen Edge*, 1998.

Taylor, A., *Castles of Cambridgeshire*. Sound archaeological surveys.

Thomas, H. M., 'The Gesta Herewardi, the English and their Conquerors', *A.N.S.* 21, 1998. Looks at the real purposes of the author of the *Gesta Herewardi* who attempts to recover for the English their reputation as fighting men.

Thorndike, Russell, *The First Englishman*. No date. A good read which bears no relation to the facts.

Van Houts, E., 'Hereward and Flanders', *Anglo-Saxon England* 28, 1999. Establishes the reality which lies behind the account of Hereward in Flanders.

Victoria County History; Vol. 1 for most eastern counties, Vol. 2 for Lincolnshire & Vol. 4 for Cambridgeshire. These studies provide much local material not found elsewhere.

Von Feilitzen, O., *The Pre-Conquest Names of Domesday Book*. Uppsala, 1937. An etymological study which casts light on the possible identity of some of Hereward's men.

Walker, D., 'The Normans in Britain'. *Historical Association Studies*, No. 1195. A useful introductory study.

Wawn, A., 'Hereward, the Danelaw and the Victorians' in *Vikings and the Danelaw* (ed. Graham Campbell, J. and others). Oxford, 2001. A study of Victorian ideas about Hereward.

Wedgewood, I., *Fenland Rivers*. Rich & Cowan, 1936. Further accounts of the changes in river systems.

Weenolson, H., *The Last Englishman; the story of Hereward the Wake*. London, 1952. An idiosyncratic novel bearing little or no resemblance to the Hereward story whatsoever.

Williams, A., *The English and the Norman Conquest*. Woodbridge, 1995. A valuable study of the survival of the English under the Normans.

Wood, M., *Domesday*. B.B.C. Classics, 1999. A useful survey of the importance of Domesday Book.

Young, M., 'History as Myth; Charles Kingsley's Hereward the Wake', *Studies in the Novel* Vol. 17, 1985. Exposes Kingsley's book as one of a genre common in Victorian times and initiated by Bulwer Lytton, the 'last days' novel.

Author of *1066*: 'A gripping re-evaluation of
those turbulent times' *THE MAIL ON SUNDAY*

Edward *the* Confessor

King of England

PETER REX

Also available from Amberley Publishing

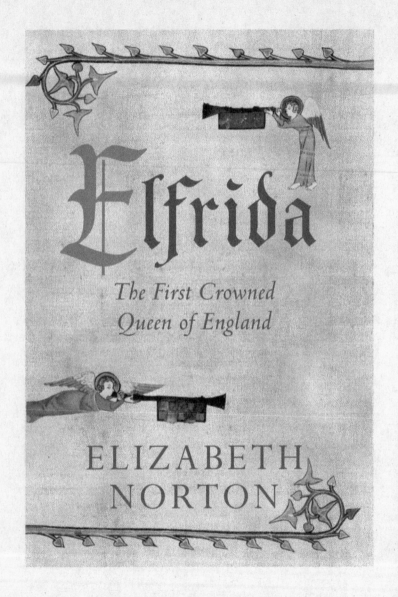

Elfrida

The First Crowned Queen of England

ELIZABETH NORTON

Also available as an ebook
Available from all good bookshops or to order direct
Please call **01453-847-800**
www.amberleybooks.com

Also available from Amberley Publishing

'A gripping re-evaluation of those turbulent times'
THE MAIL ON SUNDAY

PETER REX

1066

A New History of the Norman Conquest

A radical retelling of one of the most important events in English history

'A gripping re-evaluation of those turbulent times… Rex vividly conjures up the ebb and flow of the
battle' THE MAIL ON SUNDAY

Peter Rex tells the whole story of the Conquest of England by the Normans from its genesis in the
deathbed decision of King Edward the Confessor in January 1066 to recommend Harold Godwinson as
his successor, to the crushing of the last flickers of English resistance in June 1076.